MAKING MONEY WITH MUTUAL FUNDS

Investment Strategies to Beat the Market

WERNER RENBERG

JEREMIAH BLITZER

WILEY

John Wiley & Sons

New York · Chichester · Brisbane · Toronto · Singapore

Library of Congress Cataloging in Publication Data:

Renberg, Werner.
    Making money with mutual funds: investment strategies to
beat the market/Werner Renberg, Jeremiah Blitzer.
    p.   cm.
    Bibliography: p.
    Includes index.
    ISBN 0-471-85555-3
    1. Mutual funds.   I. Blitzer, Jeremiah. II. Title.

HG4530.R46 1988
332.63'27—dc19   87-26366
                                            CIP

Printed in the United States of America
10 9 8 7 6 5 4 3 2 1

MAKING MONEY
WITH
MUTUAL FUNDS

To the memory of

Herman & Anna Renberg
and
Moses & Clara Blitzer

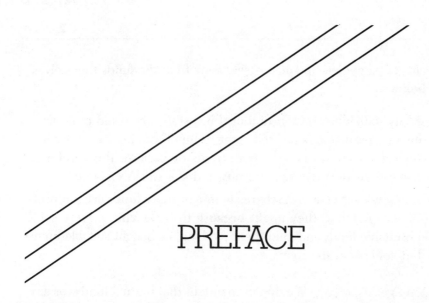

PREFACE

The attractiveness of mutual fund investment as a means of building capital—instead of, or in addition to, direct investment in stocks and bonds—is known to many.

According to the Investment Company Institute, 20 million households owned shares in the more than 1500 stock and bond funds in existence in mid-1987. According to the Federal Reserve System, purchases of mutual fund shares accounted for 44% of households' net acquisition of all financial assets in 1986—up from 5% in 1982 and almost as much as their additions to bank accounts, time deposits, and money market funds combined.

Banks, businesses, pension plans, and other institutional investors have increasingly bought mutual fund shares to attain their goals. These shares now account for more than a quarter of the assets of stock and bond funds.

Yet, despite the record volume of fund share purchases, the increased coverage of funds by the print and electronic media, and the streams of pamphlets and advertising copy from the funds themselves, we believe

- Many individuals and institutional investors who could profit from owning fund shares are reluctant to buy them because they feel they don't know enough about funds or because they prefer to make their own decisions to buy and sell stocks or bonds.
- Many who already own shares in one or more funds are not profiting as much as they might because they bought (or were sold) unsuitable funds and held them too long, or bought suitable funds but sold them too soon.

Don't get us wrong. We do not maintain that mutual funds, or any other type of financial assets, are for everyone. Nor do we pretend that any book, stockbroker, financial planner, money manager, friend, or relative can unfailingly tip you to funds that will guarantee you the maximum return on your money, year after year, under all market conditions—including a collapse as severe as the one which occurred in October 1987.

But we are convinced that investing in well-managed mutual funds could be more rewarding for more people over the long run. Perhaps they could help *you* to make more money, too—whether for yourself, your family, or the organization for which you have responsibility.

If this is what you would like to do, the main problem you face is that there are so many funds competing for your money but relatively few whose records indicate that they merit your trust.

We decided to write this book because we feel that you would prefer to manage your own fund investments if you could master the skills required to achieve your investment objectives while taking *no unnecessary risks*. You can! Toward that end, we offer suggestions on how to identify and invest in superior funds at moderate risk, in modest increments, and at low cost, and explain how to manage a fund portfolio in relatively little time.

Our book assumes neither previous fund experience nor financial training, but we believe it can be profitably utilized by people who have such background. After guiding you in selecting your first fund and judging its performance, the book helps you to develop your skills to choose additional funds that are suitable for you when the time is right.

Although many people buy fund shares from stockbrokers or other salespeople and pay commissions for advice and/or other services, we believe that you can enjoy satisfactory results by dealing with funds directly, doing your own research, making your own decisions, and paying low or no sales charges.

All you need are: a general grasp of what makes funds tick; an understanding of the sorts of funds that are appropriate for someone your age with your investment objectives, financial circumstances, and risk tolerance; and guidelines on how to find these funds. You'll find the fundamentals right here.

We begin with a chapter dealing with the relevant aspects of financial planning. We know that you are concerned about risks—the risk of losing more money than you can afford by having to sell when prices are down and the risk of losing purchasing power to inflation. Therefore, we discuss how to control your exposure to both.

We then give you an overview of the mutual fund universe to help you to understand how funds operate, and review the history (including events that no one can be proud of) so that you can view funds and current or future fund developments in a longer-run perspective.

This material is followed by the how-to chapters. We begin by outlining our strategy for selecting your first fund. We then offer suggestions for adding to your portfolio, cautioning against getting carried away and investing in too many funds: Each fund belongs in your portfolio for a reason, and you shouldn't own extra funds any more than a jigsaw puzzle should contain an extra piece. Next comes a chapter on judging your funds' performance and managing your portfolio. For those with larger assets or with pension or endowment responsibilities, a chapter on managing fund holdings through a market cycle follows. Dealing with valuation concepts to reward investors as equity leadership rotates, this chapter discusses techniques to maximize the benefits of being invested with the most qualified fund

managers at a given point in the cycle. We conclude with a chapter
that focuses on the use of mutual funds in individual retirement accounts (IRAs) and a glossary.

The October 1987 plunge in stock prices illustrated that market
risk is, of course, ever present—even for owners of shares in the most
conservatively managed funds (or the strongest corporations).

The plunge also illustrated the importance of taking a long-term
approach when investing—remaining focused on basic principles despite widespread despair or enthusiasm—and of deliberately matching
the risk level of one's portfolio with one's tolerance for risk.

Fortunately, it is not necessary to experience a sharp drop in the
stock market to understand and delimit the exposure to risk that in-
heres in your investment in any fund or group of funds. You can build
a portfolio consisting of funds whose volatility—that is, whose suscep-
tibility to falling and rising stock prices—has been measured, is some-
what predictable, and is right for you. We'll show you how to do this.

Unlike mutual fund investors in earlier years, you have the benefit
of periodic reports by a number of rating services and publications
that track the performance of most funds, as well as improved media
coverage of fund management, to supplement the increased volumes
of data that funds are required to disseminate. We suggest how you
can obtain the necessary information without spending too much
money or time. You will see that you do not need to make important
investment decisions, which can affect your and your family's financial
wellbeing for years, on the basis of self-serving pamphlets, advertising,
and sales pitches!

We could not have produced this work without the help of a number
of people who served as sounding boards for some of our thoughts,
provided statistical and other information, and cooperated in countless
other ways. Richard R. Schmaltz, Thomas Forbath, and Ronald J.
DiPrinzio—investment professionals and old friends—provided an
invaluable service by giving their counsel whenever asked to judge
our concepts and never hesitating to offer challenges. For responding
cheerfully and thoroughly to questions, and for providing and interpreting data, we express our thanks to Ann S. Anderson and Michael

W. Delaney of the Investment Company Institute; John Markese of the American Association of Individual Investors; Henry Shilling of Lipper Analytical Services; staff members of the Securities and Exchange Commission, Internal Revenue Service, and Federal Reserve System; and the many executives of mutual funds who provided useful background on their own organizations and the industry. We also wish to record our appreciation to the librarians of the New York University Graduate School of Business Administration, the SEC, and the ICI for their assistance in making reference sources available.

In expressing our gratitude for the cooperation we received from all, identified and anonymous, we do not absolve ourselves from responsibility for any inadvertent errors.

Last, but surely not least, we wish to acknowledge the steadfast support and enthusiastic encouragement of Marion Blitzer and Dalia—as well as Dan and Gil—Renberg which have been indispensable. They not only acquiesced in our dedication over many months to the work at hand, which frequently deprived them of our companionship and our help with tasks customarily ours, but also tolerated the stacks of prospectuses and reports which obstructed their view of us in our respective homes.

As we entrust these words to the compositor, permit us to express the sincere wish that you will not only profit from these pages but will also find investing in your future enjoyable.

WERNER RENBERG
JEREMIAH BLITZER

Chappaqua, New York
New York, New York
October 1987

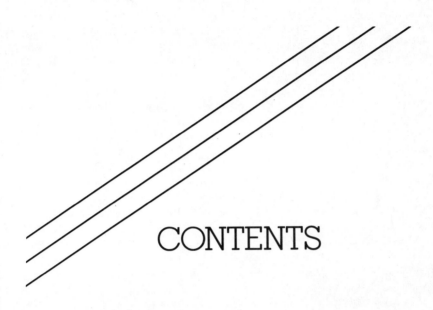

CONTENTS

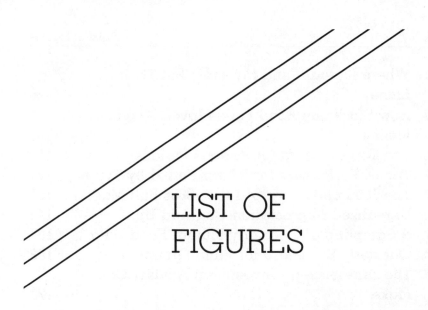

LIST OF
FIGURES

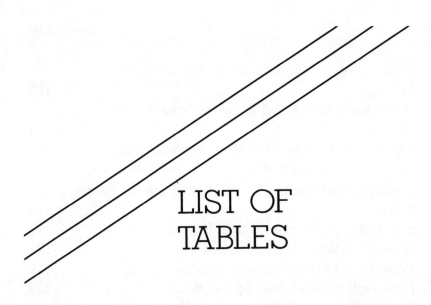

LIST OF TABLES

MAKING MONEY
WITH
MUTUAL FUNDS

INTRODUCTION

We don't know you, but we have a pretty good idea why you bought (or borrowed) this book. You probably are one of millions who:

1. . . . have reached the point in life when you think you should consider investing in some kind of securities for the first time and want to determine whether one or more mutual funds would be right for you. Or . . .

2. . . . have invested only in stocks, have profited only a little or even lost money, and want to see whether buying mutual fund shares might be more rewarding. Or . . .

3. . . . have already invested in one or more mutual funds, have not fared as well as you had hoped, find it hard to choose

1

from among the hundreds of other funds—many of them claiming
superior performance—and want to see whether our approach might
help you to do better.

If we've identified you correctly, or if you fall into some other category with a similar motivation, we believe that you're on the right
track.
This book is for you if:

You have goals—such as retirement, children's education, a business of your own, or a more luxurious home—for which you need
large amounts of money.

You understand that building your capital requires investing in securities that should keep you well ahead of inflation—stocks with
a potential for higher prices and dividends—to complement savings at more or less fixed interest rates.

You appreciate that *all* forms of savings and investment entail *some*
kind of risk.

You're willing to look at an investment approach that, reflecting
the inescapable acceptance of a reasonable degree of risk to make
money, is devised to control exposure to risk.

You're able to set aside a portion of current income for investment
each year—whether it's the $2,000 you may put into an individual
retirement account (IRA) or more.*

You're still far enough away from your goals—say, at least five
years—to see the stock market through a complete cycle to its next
peak.

You have the discipline to stay with the approach, whether during
the euphoria of a bull market, when you may be tempted to make

---

*If you're not employed, but already have a sum of capital that you want to enlarge—from an
inheritance, a former employer's savings plan, or other source—you'll also find much useful
background material and advice in this book.

a killing on some "sure thing," or during the gloom of a bear market, when you may wonder if you should sell everything.

Equity mutual funds—that is, mutual funds which are totally, primarily, or partially invested in common stocks—have inherent advantages that should help you to realize your goals. Most importantly, they offer diversification among industries and companies to reduce market risk—greater diversification than the portfolios of stocks that most people can afford or are likely to accumulate. They also provide you professional stock selection and portfolio management, the benefits of lower brokerage commission rates that institutional investors enjoy, and convenience in buying, selling, and record keeping.

To get started, you often only need $1,000—less if you're opening an IRA—and can make subsequent investments of as little as $100. Some funds have even lower minimums or none at all.

If, as we advocate, you concentrate on funds which do not impose charges when you buy and sell their shares, the advantages of mutual fund investing should cost you only an annual management fee of around 1% of the assets being managed. (There probably will be times when, using our criteria, you will identify funds that are outstanding performers but do have low sales charges. They may be worth the additional cost.)

Our approach to investing in equity mutual funds is relatively simple to execute, disciplined, and potentially profitable. Objective data should signal possible slippage in a fund manager's touch so that you can switch in time and preserve your capital. Our aim is to produce gratifying results over time, but not overnight.

You occasionally may have heard stories of stock selection leading to overnight wealth, and some of them may even have been true. It is improbable, however, that such good fortune can be repeated often enough to form the basis for a capital-building plan that you can count on. Inevitably, reaching for an exceptionally high return entails risks that are higher than you'd probably wish to take.

We suggest a strategy that moderates risk to a level that, we hope, you'll feel comfortable with. We also suggest how, after gaining experience and sharpening your skills, you might adjust the risk level of your fund portfolio to raise your expected rate of return, if you wish.

Through disciplined periodic investing of a fixed sum, regardless of market conditions, our approach helps to suppress the temptation to try the impossible: perfect market timing. When stocks are rising, your money will buy fewer shares. When stocks are falling, you pick up more. This is a widely used technique known as dollar-cost averaging, and we'll illustrate how you can profit from it.

As described in Chapter 4, our mutual fund investment strategy should keep you not only ahead of inflation but also ahead of the performance records of most professional portfolio managers. In numerical terms, it has essentially two long-term goals:

> In years when stock prices are up, your performance should match those of the top 25% of the 800–900 equity mutual funds. (We can't promise that your performance will match those of the top 1% of funds, and neither can anyone else.)

> In years when stock prices are down, your fund portfolio should outperform the Standard & Poor's 500 Composite Stock Price Index.* (From 1977 through 1986, there were two such years: 1977, when the S&P 500 total return—that is, the sum of the price change and reinvested dividends—was down about 7%, and 1981, when it fell about 5%.)

We'll show you what to look for when you consider which mutual funds you could trust with your money. Once you understand the important criteria by which to judge them, you'll be able to identify funds whose records and characteristics indicate they may be right for you.

---

*The S&P 500, whose total market value represents about 80% of the total market value of common stocks traded on the New York Stock Exchange, is designed to provide investors with a representative measure of stock market performance. It is used by many professional portfolio managers as a yardstick for periodically assessing their and others' results. You'll be using it, too.

Our recommended process for fund selection is aimed at culling, from the rapidly growing number of funds with their bewildering array of categories, those that have better prospects for participating in gains when stock prices are rising and, even more important, for not giving up those gains—and possibly more—when prices are falling, as inevitably they will.

Since there are comparatively few of these for you to consider, you can expect to make investment decisions on the basis of relatively few data, instead of basing them on the many statistics for a larger number of corporations that you'd probably be looking at if you were buying their stocks directly.

Getting the requisite information will involve only a modest amount of research in key periodicals and reference works, as well as in the prospectuses and recent reports of the funds you're focusing on. Since most of them have toll-free 800 telephone numbers, getting the fund publications you'll need will be free as well as easy. (While you have fund personnel on the phone, you should also ask them certain questions.)

You'll have no need to study companies or industries or, for that matter, economic conditions. Such analyses as are necessary are conducted by the professional staffs of the funds' investment advisers. They don't only have more time to do the research than is available to investors who have other occupations; they also possess skills and information resources which most individual investors don't have and can't easily get. Better mutual funds are run by portfolio managers who earned their records by assimilating all the information they deem essential, interpreting it correctly most of the time, and acting on it. Managers who have long records of superior results are qualified to be (indirectly) your financial consultants. Paying 1% or so of your fund assets each year for their portfolio management services won't seem excessive.

Having invested, you certainly will want to monitor your mutual funds to see whether your capital is building up at about the rate you had expected. Although it is quite possible that you can stay with your initial fund choices and continue to buy their shares for a few years, you don't want to take this likelihood for granted.

You'll want to check their performance weekly—30 minutes or so every weekend should suffice—and do a bit more every three months, when certain quarterly statistics are issued. Chapter 6 will tell you how to use easily obtained and understood information to spot changes in a fund's characteristics or behavior which might imply that you'd want to switch out of it, thereby triggering the selection process anew.

While this book is primarily aimed at individual investors—single and married, employed, self-employed, and non-working—who wish to provide for themselves and their families, we believe that portions may be useful to a good number of institutional investors as well. Pension plan managers and others who have the need to manage financial assets for the long run in a way that not only satisfies requirements for prudence but also is cost-effective will find that superior mutual funds can be as suitable a vehicle for them as they are for individuals with less money to invest.

In our writing, we have made the assumption that, despite their popularity, not everyone is yet familiar with mutual funds. Thus, of necessity, some of the material may seem elementary to those of you who have already owned fund shares. If that's the case with you, we sincerely believe, however, that you may find new ways of looking at some familiar aspects of fund investing, or perhaps discover new points which could enhance the profitability of your future investment decisions.

1

PUTTING YOUR MONEY TO WORK: BASIC STEPS TO INTELLIGENT FINANCIAL PLANNING

To say that you want to invest to make money may be accurate, but it's also inadequate. Investing has to have a focus—that is, one or more goals which require a lot of money and which you want to realize by some year(s) in the future. The number of years in which your money might work for you should be large enough to minimize the short-term risks of loss that always inhere in investing.

Lest we be misunderstood, we should make our definition clear: We're referring to investing in securities—principally common stocks and bonds—not savings.

SAVINGS FIRST

Savings, to be certain, come first. Those are the funds that constitute your emergency reserve—money to sustain your family if you're laid off and can't quickly find a new job (an all-too-common occurrence during U.S. industry's restructuring of the 1980s), to pay medical and hospital bills if a family member is stricken with an exceedingly costly illness, or to provide for some other unforeseen event. Financial planners commonly recommend that such a reserve should equal three to six months' income; how much is appropriate for you is something you can decide better than anyone else.

This money, which you cannot afford to lose, should be entrusted to taxable or tax-exempt money market funds, commercial banks, savings and loan associations, savings banks, credit unions, or the U.S. Treasury (for savings bonds).

With all of these, your principal should be safe. Your choice among them should be based on the competitiveness of their interest rates, your income tax bracket (including state and local), and your ability to get your money—without penalty for early withdrawal—when you need it.

During periods of appreciable increases in the cost of living, the sensitivity of money market funds' interest rates to market fluctuations tends to make them especially attractive. At such times, alternative savings instruments may be less competitive because laws, regulations, and the financial institutions' policies may inhibit increases in the rates they offer.

The federal government's deposit insurance or guarantee is available for essentially all but the money market funds sponsored by mutual fund families. This lack should not alarm you, however, as the safety record of money market mutual funds has been good. (If you choose one of these, check the fund's prospectus for its investment policy and the quality of its investments. If you prefer, choose a money market fund that invests only in government or insured securities. Given the reduced risk, you have to be content, of course, with a slightly lower yield.)

YOUR LONG-TERM GOALS

After you have provided adequate savings for your family and yourself, you can really begin to think of long-term goals and their attainment. Most people of working age have at least one. The nature, number, and costs of such goals depend on individual circumstances: whether you're single or married, have children or not, are employed or self-employed, own or rent your home, and have interests beyond your job.

Your goal may be to retire early, to retire at the normal age of 65 but with significantly more income than your employer's pension plan and Social Security benefits would provide, to pay for university tuition for one or more children, to start a business, to buy a home, to buy a second home, to help a child to buy a house or apartment, and so on.

The goal may require you to build an amount of capital by some date, when it will be invested for income to generate an annual cash flow that you'll have to rely on for years, or when it will be invested in physical assets (such as a house or a business). Or your goal may necessitate building a sum for the purpose of spending it (on tuition, for instance).

Retirement

If you're thinking of ensuring comfortable—or more comfortable—retirement years, you're not alone. The desire for sufficient retirement income is perhaps the most universally cited investment objective, and that's not surprising. Many—perhaps most—people do not expect their Social Security and pension checks alone to take care of their retirement needs. Even those whose employers also provide defined contribution plans, such as profit sharing or savings, may be concerned that they will fall short.

For one thing, people who long have been paying Social Security taxes have had good reason to wonder whether the Social Security system would still be solvent when they retired. And even when assured that the system had been preserved through higher taxes, many have worried whether their benefits would be reduced or even eliminated because they earned "too much money" from part-time work and/or because a portion of the Social Security payments themselves was subject to income tax.

The adequacy of an employer's pension plan is the other major cause for concern. If you've spent essentially all of your career with one company, and if that company is committed to paying you a pension according to a common formula, you may expect a year's pension checks to equal about one-half of your last annual rate of pay. (At lower salaries, the percentage would be higher; at higher salaries, it would be lower.) If the company is a truly enlightened one, it periodically will raise the amount by at least a fraction of the cumulative inflation rate.

These are big "ifs." Voluntarily or involuntarily, you may switch employers. If you don't stay with an employer long enough for pension rights to be vested, you get nothing from that company. (Most pension plans have required 10 years of service, but as a result of the Tax Reform Act of 1986 employees will be entitled to at least some pension after 5 years, beginning in 1989.) And you may get little from the next employer even if you stay. Even if you're vested before quitting or being laid off, the size of your pension may be small.

Vesting can be academic in the cases of companies that terminate pension plans or that have inadequately funded their pension programs. In cases involving defined benefit pension plans, in which the federal government's Pension Benefit Guaranty Corporation looks after employees' interests, you'd get some money, but it would not necessarily be all that you've been led to expect.

And as for inflation adjustments for those who get pensions, they usually do not come close to maintaining your purchasing power with the passing years. If you live long enough, the pension that seemed reasonable in relation to your household budget at retirement may ultimately become quite inadequate.

If you have any lingering questions as to whether you should ensure your own future or put your faith in a currently paternalistic corporation, consider a 1986 survey of corporate chief executives. As many as 84% agreed that employees should take more responsibility for providing their own retirement income.

Tuition

Few responsibilities give parents greater pride than helping a son or daughter to attend a good university or college. Paying for part, if not all, of the tuition and other costs has often meant sacrifice, but it has been the sort of sacrifice parents have cheerfully accepted.

If you're looking forward to playing this parental role, you will find, if you haven't already heard, the burden on family budgets is becoming greater each year. Universities and colleges have been raising their fees at rates exceeding that of inflation, while parents' wages or salaries, at best, have only kept even. Financial aid, which had helped to bridge the gap for many, has become more difficult to obtain. (The Tax Reform Act of 1986 implicitly encourages homeowners to borrow against their homes for purposes such as tuition. If, like many others, you're happy to be *reducing* your mortgage, you'll recoil at the thought— and cost—of piling a new layer of debt on your home.)

Buying a Home

Except in the case of pressing need, you do not *have* to buy a house or apartment in a given year. But in view of the continuing increase in housing prices—outside of areas that are temporarily depressed—

you'll usually find it prudent to buy as soon as you have the money for a down payment, mortgage debt service, and property taxes. Upgrading by moving to a higher-income community or more luxurious house is even less likely to be a matter of urgency, but it, too, is better undertaken sooner rather than later.

If you have some discretion as to when to buy, compare the rate of increase of home prices in your area with the rates of return you're likely to get from your investments. It's important to know which is greater. If housing prices are stable but you can get a good return on your money, you may be able to plan investments so that you can afford a better house or a larger down payment. If housing prices are on the run and securities markets are flat or falling, you may not have time to build your capital. It may make more sense to buy a house that offers less than the house you had dreamed of—and plan to upgrade after it has appreciated for a few years.

PUTTING A PRICE TAG ON YOUR GOALS

Whatever your long-term goals—whether among those mentioned or not—you have to make rough estimates of how much money you'll need and in what years you'll need it.

A critical element in such calculation is the probable rate of inflation for the period between now and the year(s) you'll want the money. Knowing what rate to use for a long period of years is not easy. As surveys by *The Wall Street Journal* demonstrate twice a year, some of the most distinguished economists in the country can't predict the change in the consumer price index (CPI) correctly six months in advance. They often can't even get the *direction* of the change right. How can you, then, expect to know the rate by which the CPI will rise over a period of years?

The easiest thing for you to do would be to adopt a plausible rate used in a long-term forecast by a well-regarded economist, and watch to see whether it is revised. Alternatively, you could assume extension of a recent trend, if that makes sense, but check periodically if the trend changes. (For the years 1982 through 1986, the average annual increase in the consumer price index was a bit above 3%.)

Thus, if you're contemplating having capital for specific outlays in specific years, you'll take these steps: Get an idea of how much you would need today for the same purpose(s), and apply the projected inflation rate to estimate the approximate annual costs in the years for which you're planning.

You may find it desirable to use a rate higher or lower than the inflation rate. For example, you may want to assume that recent trends of *above*-inflation increases in tuition costs will continue indefinitely. (If a good school could cost $10,000 to $15,000 in the mid-1980s, only a 5% annual increase could raise this range to $16,000 to $24,000 in 10 years.) And you know the cost will rise each year your child (children) is (are) in school.

A considerably trickier calculation is the one to estimate how much capital you'll need by the time you retire so that you can invest in a way that assures you sufficient supplementary income. The process, greatly simplified, goes something like this:

1. Determine as well as you can how much your expected pension and Social Security checks are likely to bring in each year over your expected lifetime and, if you're married, that of your spouse. This will require educated guesses as to how close the checks are likely to come to matching increases in the cost of living.

2. Estimate what your living costs are likely to be during your retirement years. This requires adding up your current annual costs by categories—ignoring those, such as commuting, which will not continue after you stop working—and applying an inflation rate for each year of your projection. Although it is easier to apply the same rate across the board, you may want to treat different categories differently. (Mortgage debt service may be fixed. Property taxes may go up less than the inflation rate. Health care, an increasingly important item as we get older, may rise at a rate faster than general inflation.) You may want

to fatten some categories—with more time for travel, you may
want to allow for higher vacation expenditures, for example.

3. For each year of your projection, calculate whether your after-
    tax pension and Social Security payments (and any other income
    you may expect) fall short of your expected living costs and, if
    so, by how much. It is this shortfall that you'll try to make up
    with income from the capital sum you want to accumulate and
    from any other financial assets you already have working for
    you.

Knowing how much after-tax money you will need to depend on
each year to maintain your standard of living, you'll be able to figure
out how much capital would have to be invested at a given rate to
earn it.

INVESTING TO REACH YOUR GOALS

How can you build the amount of capital you'll need for retirement
or other purposes? As you'll see, all it takes are time and money—
accompanied by patience and the willingness to take deliberate risk.
We'll begin by demonstrating how time and money can work for you.

The Power of Compounding

For purposes of discussion, let's assume that you will need $100,000
in some distant year and you want to generate that sum by investing
a fixed amount annually and by reinvesting all the income earned as
it's credited to you.

Table 1-1 shows how you can accumulate $100,000 by investing
various sums to earn compound rates of return of 5%, 10%, and 15%
for different periods. (These rates may or may not be available to you.
We're using them only for illustration.) To keep the calculation simple,
we have made no provision for income taxes. In the real world, unfortunately, you'd have to do that, of course, unless you could get
these rates in tax-exempt securities.

TABLE 1-1. Annual Investment Requirements to Accumulate $100,000

Number of Years	Sums to be Invested Annually at		
	5%	10%	15%
5	$18,098	$16,380	$14,832
10	7,951	6,275	4,925
15	4,634	3,147	2,102
20	3,024	1,746	976
25	2,095	1,017	470

Note: No provision is made for possible income tax liabilities.

Note how, thanks to the power of compounding, the required annual sums drop off sharply when you're able to invest over longer periods—an advantage best exploited when one is young. Note that the opposite is also true: When you have fewer years and/or less money to invest, you need to earn a higher return to build the same amount of capital. That could mean you'd have to incur greater risk than might be appropriate for you under the circumstances.

Before going on, you may wish to practice calculating the amounts, periods, and rates of return that are closer to the ones in your case. A hand calculator with a compounding key will make it easy to compare possible scenarios. You also may wish to introduce the probable income tax rates to which you'd be exposed.

Having seen how time, money, and rates of return interact, let's take a look at each of these.

Time for Investment

The time that your money can work for you may or may not be within your control. The time until you retire at the normal age of 65 or until your child (children) goes (go) to college, for example, is essentially fixed. The time until early retirement may be subject to your discretion or it may be essentially dictated to you by your employer. On the other hand, the period until you make a major purchase—a vacation home, a business, and so on—is more a matter of choice.

Whatever your goals and whatever time is involved in your planning, you have to bear a basic principle in mind: The risk inherent in any investment—indeed, the probability that its market value may fall below your cost—declines with time. The more years you have available for money to work for you, the more stable the average annual rate of return on your investment becomes, and the greater the opportunity you have to incur higher risks in hopes of earning higher returns. As your time horizon shrinks, so does your choice of suitable investments.

Money for Investment

We can add little to what you know about your ability to invest a certain sum annually. You will have to determine how much money you are able to spare regularly out of your expected income from employment, self-employment, and/or other sources. But, on the other hand, this may be an opportune time to analyze your spending to see whether it could be trimmed without real sacrifice. Cutting your household budget by only $20 a week could make $1,000 available for investment every year. If applied annually for 10 years to buy shares of a mutual fund with an average return of 15%, the savings would grow to about $20,000—enough, one hopes, to pay for a year's university tuition, room, and board.

In making your estimates of income and outgo, you will want to be sure that investing a constant sum periodically will not force you to reduce your standard of living or to tap your savings, which should be maintained at adequate levels to cover emergency needs. (The last thing you want is to run the risk of having to suspend your investment program or even to sell investments when prices are depressed.)

If you find that you are able to invest the requisite amount—based on your expected time horizon and rate of return—out of income, good. If not, you will have to moderate your goal(s), extend the time by which you plan to attain it (them), and/or raise the level of risk which you would incur.

If you're lucky enough to be able to invest annually more than your estimated investment requirements, you can, of course, reduce the risk level of your investments, accelerate the speed with which you expect to attain your goal(s), and/or enlarge your goal(s).

Rates of Return

Once you know how much you can invest and for how long you can invest it, you can reckon what compound rate of return your investments must earn to let you reach your objective(s).

Table 1-2 illustrates the range of pretax compound annual rates of return required to accumulate $100,000, depending on the rates of annual investment and the number of years of investing. Some of the returns are clearly unattainable. In fact, the rate you can count on being attainable over the long run may be lower than you imagine.

TABLE 1-2. Annual Rates of Return Required to Accumulate $100,000

Annual Investment	Number of Years			
	5	10	15	20
$ 2,400	119.28%	29.54%	13.37%	7.15%
4,800	75.80	15.53	4.53	0.43
7,200	52.83	7.11	----	----
9,600	37.38	0.90	----	----
12,000	25.78	----	----	----
14,400	16.49	----	----	----
16,800	8.73	----	----	----

Note: No provision is made for possible income tax liabilities.

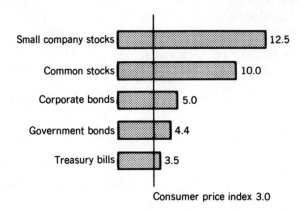

Figure 1-1. Annual Rates of Return for Select Financial Assets 1926–86. Data source: Roger G. Ibbotson and Rex A. Sinquefield, *Stocks, Bonds, Bills and Inflation,* 1982 edition (Institute for Chartered Financial Analysts, Charlottesville, Va.), updated in *Stocks, Bonds, Bills and Inflation: 1987 Yearbook* (Ibbotson Associates, Chicago).

Figure 1-1 shows the compound annual rates earned by certain financial assets over the 61-year period, 1926–86, according to an analysis published by Ibbotson Associates.

You may not be planning to invest for 61 years, but the Ibbotson data are relevant to you nonetheless.*

The data should reassure you by showing that positive rates were earned by financial assets over this long period—all exceeding the long-term inflation rate of 3.0%—despite wars, the Great Depression, recessions, and other major events. By coming through in the proper textbook ranking—the most risky assets earning the highest return and the least risky, the lowest—the rates can provide comfort to those who value the little predictability that occurs in financial affairs.

*In case you're wondering, $1 invested in the S&P 500 at the start of 1926 would have grown to $330.67 by the end of 1986.

Similar relationships prevailed, but returns were higher, in the 10 years ended in 1986, as illustrated in Figure 1-2.

As you make your long-term financial plans, with memories of returns of recent years (Table 1-3) still fresh, it will be useful to keep the long-run historical record in mind. Only time will tell whether future returns—those on which *you* have to depend—will come closer to the long-run rates or the recent averages. For certain, it would be improvident to base your strategy on the assumption that high returns of recent years are likely to recur often enough to constitute a new norm.

Ibbotson data make clear why government and high grade corporate bonds, which have an aura of safety about them because of their high quality, may be questionable investments for individuals who wish to earn more than 1 to 2% after adjustment for inflation. Sure, bonds put on an impressive performance for much of the 1980s—especially

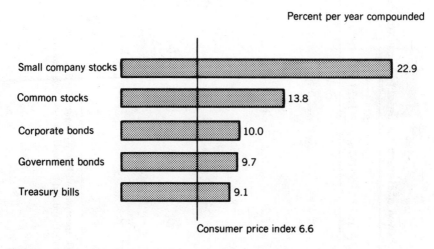

Figure 1-2. Annual Rates of Return for Select Financial Assets 1977–86. Data source: Roger G. Ibbotson and Rex A. Sinquefield, *Stocks, Bonds, Bills and Inflation*, 1982 edition (Institute for Chartered Financial Analysts, Charlottesville, Va.), updated in *Stocks, Bonds, Bills and Inflation: 1987 Yearbook* (Ibbotson Associates, Chicago).

TABLE 1-3. Rates of Return for Select Financial Assets 1977–1986

Asset	1977	1978	1979	1980	1981	1982	1983	1984	1985	1986
Small Company Stocks	25.4%	23.5%	43.5%	39.9%	13.9%	28.0%	39.7%	(6.7%)	24.7%	6.9%
S&P 500 Common Stocks	(7.2)	6.6	18.4	32.4	(4.9)	21.4	22.5	6.3	32.2	18.5
20-Year Corp. Bonds	1.7	(0.1)	(4.2)	(2.6)	(1.0)	43.8	4.7	16.4	30.9	19.8
20-Year Govt. Bonds	(0.7)	(1.2)	(1.2)	(4.0)	1.8	40.3	0.7	15.4	31.0	24.4
Treasury Bills	5.1	7.2	10.4	11.2	14.7	10.5	8.8	9.8	7.7	6.2
CPI	6.8	9.0	13.3	12.4	8.9	3.9	3.8	4.0	3.8	1.1

Source: Roger G. Ibbotson and Rex A. Sinquefield, *Stocks, Bonds, Bills and Inflation,* 1982 edition (Institute for Chartered Financial Analysts, Charlottesville, Va.), updated in *Stocks, Bonds, Bills and Inflation: 1987 Yearbook* (Ibbotson Associates, Chicago).

in 1982 and 1985—but this was a period in which interest rates fell
sharply, causing prices of bonds to soar. If you look back to the inflationary late 1970s, for example, you'll see a different picture: Bond
yields could not offset the fall in bond prices, resulting in a *negative*
total return (Table 1-4).

On the other hand, Ibbotson data affirm the belief that over the
long run one can earn significantly higher returns on common stocks
than on other financial assets. Table 1-5 shows how dividends (1) add
to return or (2) offset a significant share of a drop in stock prices. It
also makes vivid the volatility which characterizes returns on common
stocks and which makes it important, when investing in stocks, to
stay in them long enough to ride out the swings. (For more on stock
market cycles, see box, page 24.)

**TABLE 1-4. Components of Total Return for Long-Term
Government Bonds 1977–1986**

Year	Capital Appreciation	Yield	Return on Reinvestment	Total Return
1977	(7.95%)	7.85%	(0.57%)	(0.67%)
1978	(9.08)	8.64	(0.72)	(1.16)
1979	(9.79)	9.42	(0.84)	(1.22)
1980	(13.77)	11.24	(1.43)	(3.95)
1981	(10.40)	13.54	(1.30)	1.85
1982	23.86	13.56	2.93	40.35
1983	(9.92)	11.65	(1.06)	0.68
1984	2.26	12.91	0.27	15.43
1985	17.79	11.34	1.84	30.97
1986	15.16	8.25	1.03	24.44

Source: Roger G. Ibbotson and Rex A. Sinquefield, *Stocks, Bonds, Bills and Inflation*,
1982 edition (Institute for Chartered Financial Analysts, Charlottesville, Va.), updated
in *Stocks, Bonds, Bills and Inflation: 1987 Yearbook* (Ibbotson Associates, Chicago).

TABLE 1-5. Components of Total Return for Common Stocks 1977–1986

Year	Capital Appreciation	Dividend Return	Return on Reinvestment	Total Return
1977	(11.50%)	4.84%	(0.52%)	(7.18%)
1978	1.06	5.45	0.05	6.56
1979	12.31	5.50	0.64	18.44
1980	25.77	5.42	1.23	32.42
1981	(9.72)	5.29	(0.48)	(4.91)
1982	14.76	5.85	0.80	21.41
1983	17.27	4.52	0.72	22.51
1984	1.39	4.81	0.07	6.27
1985	26.34	4.71	1.11	32.16
1986	14.33	3.41	0.43	18.47

Source: Roger G. Ibbotson and Rex A. Sinquefield, *Stocks, Bonds, Bills and Inflation*, 1982 edition (Institute for Chartered Financial Analysts, Charlottesville, Va.), updated in *Stocks, Bonds, Bills and Inflation: 1987 Yearbook* (Ibbotson Associates, Chicago).

DEVELOPING A STRATEGY FOR YOU

The investment strategy which should enable you to earn your desired *total* return has to be based on the mix of financial assets that is most likely provide you the appropriate combination of capital appreciation, income, and risk.

We say "most likely" because there are few guarantees in the financial world. When dealing with marketable securities, we live with probabilities—the probabilities that rates of return for each type and grade of financial instrument will fluctuate in a distinct way, signifying varying degrees of risk and producing long-term averages such as we've noted. Your planning unavoidably must take into account the extent of the fluctuations in returns—or risk—as well as the averages.

When all is said and done, the choices for you to consider for your long-term investment strategy boil down to three categories of financial assets: cash equivalents for income and safety of principal, fixed-income securities for slightly higher income and possible capital appreciation, and common stocks for capital appreciation and some income.

Income, Capital Appreciation, and Risk

The Tax Reform Act of 1986 made life simpler, but more painful, by eliminating the preferential treatment of long-term capital gains. In erasing the distinction between capital appreciation and income from a tax standpoint (and in lowering tax rates), the Act made income from interest and dividends more attractive to those in higher brackets who heretofore may have tried to minimize them while maximizing capital gains.

Despite their new tax status, capital gains remain an important goal. If you find rates of current income from interest and/or dividends alone too low to meet your long-term objectives, you have no alternative but to seek capital gains.

Unfortunately, there is no hope of earning capital gains without incurring the risk of capital losses—a truism that people sometimes forget to their regret. No matter how bright the prospects seem for appreciation of any bonds, stocks, or shares of mutual funds which invest in them, the risk of loss is always present when one buys them. Expectations of larger gains usually entail taking larger risks.

A Comparison of Financial Assets

Common Stocks. Over time, as we've seen in this chapter, your best prospects for capital appreciation will be found, generally, in common stocks.

Not all stocks are alike, of course, because the corporations which have issued them are so different. They differ in the degree of their financial soundness, their profitability, the size and mix of their assets, the patterns of their revenue growth, and the maturity and stability of their industries, to name a few of the more obvious attributes.

STOCK MARKET CYCLES

Once when J.P. Morgan, Sr. was stopped on the street and asked what the stock market was going to do, he simply responded, "It will fluctuate." Table 1-6 does not only prove how right he was, it also proves how important it is to keep market cycles in mind when investing in common stocks—and to forget about investing if you may not be able to stay in stocks until the next market peak. Since the length and extent of bull and bear markets seem to fit no pattern, they are impossible to predict. Never knowing which way stock prices are going to go, you can never be sure if you're buying shares at the lowest price; investing by dollar-cost averaging (see Chapter 4) probably will result in as low an average price as you can hope for.

While this 58-year record of major swings in stock prices does not enable anyone to forecast stock prices, it does permit you to draw a few inferences that may be worth remembering:

- Both bull and bear markets end—sooner or later.
- Bull markets, on average, last more than twice as long.
- The length of an average peak-to-peak cycle is about six years. Three of the last four have lasted longer.
- The increase in average stock prices during an average bull market more than makes up for the average loss in the preceding bear market. That's why it is so essential, when investing in stocks, to have the time and the discipline to invest for a long enough period.

TABLE 1-6. Major Stock Price Swings (1929–1987)

		Bull Market Length in Months	Bear Market Length in Months	Percent Rise in Stock Prices*	Percent Fall in Stock Prices*
Peak	Sep. 1929	97		404.27%	
Trough	June 1932		33		86.22%
Peak	Mar. 1937	57		324.55	
Trough	Mar. 1938		12		54.50
Peak	Jan. 1939	10		53.88	
Trough	Apr. 1942		39		42.89
Peak	May 1946	49		157.70	
Trough	June 1949		37		29.61
Peak	Jan. 1953	43		96.75	
Trough	Sep. 1953		8		14.82
Peak	July 1956	34		119.02	
Trough	Oct. 1957		15.		21.63
Peak	Aug. 1959	22		55.75	
Trough	Oct. 1960		14		13.85
Peak	Nov. 1968	97		107.21	
Trough	May 1970		18		36.06
Peak	Jan. 1973	32		73.53	
Trough	Oct. 1974		21		48.20
Peak	Nov. 1980	73		125.63	
Trough	Aug. 1982		21		27.11
Peak	Aug. 1987	60		228.81	
Trough[(p)]	Oct. 1987		2		33.24
Average		52.2	20.0	158.83%	37.10%

*1929–1957, Standard & Poor's Stock Price Index; 1957–1987, S&P 500 Composite Stock Price Index.

p = preliminary

Data source: Standard & Poor's Corporation.

Prospects for capital appreciation are best—and the risks of loss least—in the stocks of companies which enjoy, and promise to continue enjoying, significant growth in profits. If the companies also pay good dividends, so much the better. Dividend-paying stocks are attractive not only because they offer both income and the potential for capital appreciation, but also because their dividends cushion the slide in their total returns during down markets.

Fixed-Income Securities. To play it safe and earn predictable income by investing in bonds* incurs risks also. The safety of bonds lies in the ability of an issuer—whether the U.S. Government or an unknown manufacturer—to repay the principal at maturity. But even if you assume that the issuer will repay on time, and thus pose no credit risk, bond investments always incur market and inflation risks.

Prices of fixed-income securities fall when interest rates rise, and they rise when interest rates fall. Those with longer maturities, which normally have higher yields than those with shorter maturities, also tend to rise and fall more. Since interest rates fluctuate continually, no one can predict with certainty the price of any fixed-income security for any date in the future—other than the price on the day it matures (or, if it's callable prior to maturity, on the day it's called). Figure 1-3 illustrates the difficulties experts have in predicting only six months ahead.

No matter which way bond prices move, they sometimes will confront you with a dilemma. When market interest rates fall and prices of outstanding bonds rise to a premium, you may be tempted to sell to capture capital gains. But when you want to reinvest the proceeds, you have to be content with a lower return. When interest rates rise and bond prices fall, you may be inclined to sell prior to maturity, accepting a known capital loss before it becomes bigger.

The exceptional performance of bonds in 1982 and 1985 notwithstanding, you cannot look to them for capital appreciation as a matter

---

*We'll ignore preferred stocks because they're essentially unsuitable for individual investors.

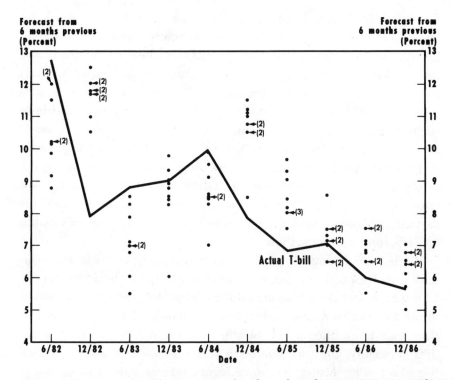

Figure 1-3. Treasury Bill Rates: Actual and Predicted. Source: *Review*, The Federal Reserve Bank of St. Louis, March 1987. Reprinted with permission. This chart compares the actual 3-month Treasury bill rate, plotted twice a year beginning in June 1982, with the six-months-ahead rate forecasts by nine economists who were surveyed regularly over this period by *The Wall Street Journal*. Not only did they fail to get the rate correctly; most of the time, they failed to predict the *direction* of change.

of course. At the least, bonds offer fixed income—with all the reassurance, and hazards, that connotes.

Beyond market risk, you need to remember the inflation risk that is associated more with bonds than with stocks. As we've noted, Ibbotson calculated that the real total return on government and corporate bonds came to about 1% per year for the entire 1926–1986 period, but during inflationary years such as 1980 and 1981, their real total returns were *negative*.

Cash Equivalents. Cash equivalents, such as U.S. Treasury bills, bank certificates of deposit (CDs), and commercial paper, provide no growth—only income. Essentially free of risk, they pay relatively low rates of interest. Although CDs are available for as long as 5 years, the maturities of cash equivalents generally run no more than a year.

Except for those who cannot or need not take any risks and only require a modest rate of return, investors typically use cash equivalents for two purposes: to earn a return on money invested temporarily while deciding where to invest it long-term, or to balance risky assets in portfolios. The money market instruments that constitute cash equivalents may be identical or similar to financial assets used for savings but, unlike savings, the money remains "in play," available for switching into securities.

While banks' longer-term CDs involve no market risk, they can have drawbacks. When money market interest rates fall, investors in CDs with longer maturities are sitting pretty. But when money market interest rates rise, CD investors can be out of luck. Locked in, unless they wish to sacrifice a few months' interest and pay an early withdrawal penalty, they are unable to switch to assets more responsive to market rates. Moreover, since higher interest rates usually imply a higher inflation rate, they also find themselves watching passively as their principal's purchasing power melts.

Your Asset Allocation

Knowing how much you are able to invest regularly, what you would like to earn by investing, and which financial assets are more suitable, you now are ready to draw up your strategy and implement it.

Choosing the mix of financial assets that's right for you depends on their expected rates of return and on your need, ability, and willingness to tolerate risk.

If your time horizon is a long one, your asset allocation can be heavily weighted to common stocks. To moderate risk, the portfolio of stocks should be diversified among 10 or so industries and complemented by a moderate share of cash equivalents.

If your time horizon is relatively short—but not too short to invest in equities—you should lighten the portion devoted to stocks, raise the level of cash equivalents, and perhaps add some bonds maturing in no more than 5 years. Although a small share is allocated to stocks, the portfolio should be just as diversified. The bonds are introduced to raise the portfolio's income; having short maturities, they will be less subject to fluctuation—or market risk—than long bonds.

Embarking on this program, you know that your initial asset allocation is not carved into granite. You know that you'll have the opportunity to change it if and when circumstances warrant.

Since you'll be investing set amounts of money at regular intervals—a technique known as dollar-cost averaging—you'll reduce the risk of buying stocks at a market peak and eliminate the frequently perceived need of market timing.

TAKING ADVANTAGE OF MUTUAL FUNDS

Now that you have an overview of a rational strategy for profitable long-term investment in financial assets, you're ready to begin putting your money to work.

Or are you?

If you were to begin to apply some of the points made in this chapter, you'd quickly discover that investing on your own isn't as easy as it may appear to be. Even if you made a preliminary decision on how to allocate your assets, found that investing in cash equivalents posed no challenge, and resorted to buying U.S. Treasury securities of short maturities, which stocks would you pick for the long term?

How long would it take you to select a diversified portfolio of approximately 10 companies whose long-term prospects you could feel confident about and which in the short run would not cause you to lose sleep? How feasible would it be, given the amount you want to invest regularly, to buy the odd numbers of shares of each stock that would enable you to put equal amounts of money into each of them?

Since brokerage commissions are higher as a percent of a transaction when you buy in odd lots, how much of your investment would they absorb?

How much effort would be required to watch your investments so that you'd know if one goes sour?

If all of this causes you to pause and makes you wonder whether you should have professional help—a financial planner or investment counselor, for example—you may soon find that if your account is big enough to interest them in the first place, their fees are high, and their investment records are not necessarily commensurate. Moreover, their advice may not be truly objective if they want to sell you financial "products" that provide them with commissions.

What do you do?

Consider mutual funds.* A strategy employing superior mutual funds can help you to attain your investment objectives much more easily than you could on your own.

Consider the advantages which mutual funds offer you:

1. They enable you to implement your asset allocation targets by offering you choices of money market, bond, and equity funds, or funds which themselves have allocated assets among cash equivalents, bonds, and stocks.

2. They make it easy for you to switch as economic conditions or your circumstances warrant changes in your allocations, or to redeem your shares at any time if you need the money.

3. They will automatically reinvest dividends and/or realized capital gains, unless you request that these be distributed to you.

4. Given their low investment requirements, you can take advantage of their diversification among stocks and bonds, easily and economically, with your first investment and each subsequent one.

---

*If you already own securities or have an interest in a company savings or stock plan, you'll want to take these into account when allocating assets.

5. Professional managers, devoting full time to the task, make and execute decisions on what to buy and sell and when to do so.

6. Although performance by the average equity fund has fallen short of the stock market averages in recent years, one out of four fund managers has outperformed the market.

7. It's possible, as we'll show, to select funds which can be expected to do well in bull markets and conserve capital in bear markets.

8. Daily quotations and other frequently disseminated, easy-to-understand data enable you to see quickly how your funds are doing. You can always know if you're on course.

9. Many funds impose only nominal charges, principally for asset management.

In the rest of this book, we'll describe the mutual fund industry, tell you what you need to know before investing in funds, give you our strategy for selecting a few well-managed equity funds out of about 900 in operation, and suggest how you should manage your fund portfolio. We'll also give you pointers about using mutual funds for individual retirement accounts.

2

LOOKING INTO MUTUAL FUNDS

Mutual funds, legally known as open-end investment companies, are corporations and trusts organized to enable investors to pool their money for the purpose of acquiring interests in managed portfolios of securities.* This contrasts with the majority of business entities which are organized to produce and sell goods and services.

The phrase "open-end" refers to mutual funds' continuous offer to sell shares to anyone who wants to buy and to redeem the shares of anyone who wants to sell—directly or via brokers or others. The number of shares which mutual funds have outstanding changes daily, in contrast with closed-

*A few were formed as limited partnerships.

end companies, or funds, which have a fixed number of shares outstanding. The outstanding shares of closed-end funds, some of which are traded on stock exchanges, are bought from people who own them as other corporations' stocks are, not from the fund organizations or their agents.

Around 2,200 open-end investment companies are registered with the Securities and Exchange Commission—including money market and municipal bond funds—permitting the sale of their shares in interstate commerce. The number continues to grow as more are created than are terminated each year.

In this book we're concerned mostly with the roughly 900 mutual funds, having more than $200 billion in net assets, which have invested partially, principally, or exclusively in common stocks. No one knows exactly how many there are at any time. The SEC does not break down totals for registered companies by types (i.e., stock funds, money market funds, government bond funds, and so on). The Investment Company Institute, the industry's trade association, only keeps data of its own members, whose assets constitute about 90% of the industry's total and whose mix is believed to be representative of the total industry.*

Before concentrating on the fraction of the 900 funds that you should primarily consider for building your capital, we want to give you an overview of the industry. In this chapter, we'll take a look at how funds are regulated, how they are organized, how they are classified, how they try to realize their various investment objectives, what it costs you to invest in them, and how you deal with them.

HOW FUNDS ARE REGULATED

In response to abuses of the 1920s and subsequent shoddy practices, the U.S. Government has enacted and occasionally amended a set of

---

*Unless attributed otherwise, fund data used throughout this book are those of ICI. Their omission of a number of funds should not invalidate conclusions that may be drawn from them.

laws to protect mutual fund investors against dishonesty—but not against falling prices or consequent losses.

The most important of the laws are the Securities Act of 1933, the Securities Exchange Act of 1934, the Investment Company Act of 1940 (the principal piece of mutual fund legislation) and the Investment Advisers Act of 1940. (States, too, have relevant regulations, but we'll skip these to concentrate on the provisions of the more important federal laws and to keep matters—well, relatively—simple.)

First and foremost, to be able to offer you its shares, a mutual fund has to register them with the SEC. To do that, a fund must file a registration statement which contains a wealth of information in three parts: a prospectus, which *has to be* given to every potential investor; a statement of additional information, which needs only to be given to every investor who requests one; and additional statements, which are submitted only to the SEC.

Reporting Requirements

The Prospectus. No single document is more important to you, as a present or potential mutual fund investor, than a fund's prospectus. Its purpose is to provide essential information about a fund in a way that will help you to make an informed decision about whether to buy its shares. Information that is of interest to some, but not essential to all, may be supplied in the statement of additional information.

Because of the importance of the document and investors' uneven tolerance or understanding of technical and legal terms, the SEC urges funds to make the prospectus prose easy to understand and brief.

Information which *must be* in a prospectus includes:

1. The type of fund or a brief statement of its investment objectives. (Figure 2-1.)
2. Condensed financial information per share for each of the last 10 years, or for the life of the fund, if shorter, such as investment income, expenses, net investment income, dividends from net investment income, net realized and unrealized gains/losses on

**The primary objective of the
Lindner Fund, Inc. is long term
capital appreciation. Income is
a secondary objective of the
Fund. Pursuant to this policy,
the Fund ordinarily will invest
substantially all of its assets in
common stocks or securi-
ties convertible into common
stocks.**

(a)

**The primary objective of the Lindner Dividend
Fund, Inc. is the production of current income.
Capital appreciation is a secondary objective of the
Fund. Pursuant to this policy, the Fund invests its
assets in common stocks yielding substantial dividend income, preferred stocks convertible or not
convertible into common stock and, to a lesser
extent, in corporate bonds and debt securities
issued or guaranteed by the United States, its
agencies or instrumentalities. The Fund defines
"substantial dividend income" as a rate of return
materially higher than that paid on either the Standard & Poor's Composite Average of 500 stocks or
on passbook savings accounts.**

(b)

Figure 2-1. An Overriding Objective: Clarity of Expression. Two funds for
which Lindner Management Corporation is investment adviser have opposite
primary investment objectives, but have another objective in common: to
satisfy the legal requirement for expressing their investment objectives
clearly.

securities, distributions from net realized gains on securities, net increase/decrease in net asset value (NAV), NAV at beginning of year, and NAV at end of year (Figure 2-2).

3. Other condensed financial information (for each of the same years): ratios of expenses to average net assets and net investment income to average net assets, portfolio turnover rate, and the number of shares outstanding at the end of the period (Figure 2-2).

   Note: If an investment adviser has been changed, the date of the change must be shown as a footnote to the financial table. This reflects the importance which is accorded the investment adviser, a subject to which we will return.

4. A description of the fund's organization and existing or proposed operation, including investment objectives and policies. It must state whether the fund is a diversified or nondiversified investment company in the eyes of the law. To be classified as diversified under the 1940 Act, a fund, among other things, must ensure that in 75% of its portfolio no one issuer's securities account for more than 5% of the total assets. (The remaining 25% could be accounted for by one issuer alone.)

   The prospectus also must note the investment objectives which management can change without a vote of the majority of shareholders, the policies—including those deemed to be fundamental—which can only be changed by a majority vote, the types of securities in which the fund will invest, any special practices or techniques which it may use (such as risk arbitrage, repurchase agreements, forward delivery contracts), any statement on concentration in a particular industry or group of industries (for this purpose, concentration is defined as 25% or more of the fund's total assets), and the principal risk factors associated with investment in the fund (Figure 2-3).

5. Names and description of the management, including the board of directors (and its responsibilities), the investment adviser (its

		Years Ended March 31,*									
		1987	1986	1985	1984	1983	1982	1981	1980	1979	1978
1.	Investment income	$ .81	$ .76	$ 1.11	$ .63	$ .44	$ .61	$ .80	$ .66	$ .36	$ .30
2.	Expenses	.39	.27	.32	.26	.11	.23	.30	.22	.18	.13
3.	Investment income—net	.42	.49	.79	.37	.33	.38	.50	.44	.18	.17
4.	Dividends from investment income—net	(.46)	(.65)	(.37)	(.26)	(.33)	(.58)	(.39)	(.17)	(.16)	(.12)
5.	Realized and unrealized gain (loss) on investments—net	11.39	19.59	5.75	2.73	15.80	(.02)	14.46	2.17	3.99	1.43
6.	Distributions from realized gain on investments—net	(6.84)‡	(1.78)	(3.69)	(1.88)	(1.23)	(9.92)	(.13)	—	—	—
7.	Net increase (decrease) in net asset value	4.51	17.65	2.48	.96	14.57	(10.14)	14.44	2.44	4.01	1.48
	Net asset value:										
8.	Beginning of year	55.34	37.69	35.21	34.25	19.68	29.82	15.38	12.94	8.93	7.45
9.	End of year	$59.85	$55.34	$37.69	$35.21	$34.25	$19.68	$29.82	$15.38	$12.94	$8.93
10.	Ratio of expenses to average net assets	1.08%	1.08%	1.12%	1.04%	.85%	1.34%	1.23%	1.40%	1.52%	1.60%
11.	Ratio of investment income—net to average net assets	1.18%	1.95%	2.79%	1.47%	2.56%	2.39%	2.08%	2.77%	1.49%	2.03%
12.	Portfolio turnover rate†	96%	96%	126%	85%	120%	194%	277%	338%	249%	238%
13.	Shares outstanding at end of period (000 omitted)	165,230	109,975	62,716	45,757	23,403	5,896	1,971	2,096	2,358	2,598

* Adjusted for a 3 for 1 split paid December 19, 1980.

† In accordance with a Securities and Exchange Commission's rules amendment, portfolio turnover rates after 1984 include U.S. Government long-term securities which were excluded from the calculations in prior years.

‡ Includes a special interim distribution of $2.85 per share, paid in December 1986, from gain on investments—net realized during the fiscal year ended March 31, 1987.

Figure 2-2. Ten Years of Per-Share Data. This table from Fidelity's Magellan Fund prospectus provides the information required to show how its net asset value changed over a decade as well as other information to enable investors to judge the fund.

38

Investment Objective and Policies

The Fund is an open-end, diversified, management investment company which was incorporated in Delaware in March 1970. The primary investment objective of the Fund is long-term growth of capital. The Fund's investment objective is a fundamental policy which cannot be changed without shareholder approval. Income is not a specific objective, although it is anticipated that long-term growth of capital will be accompanied by growth of income.

The Fund attempts to achieve its objective by investing at least 80% of the value of its assets in a diversified portfolio of common stocks and securities convertible into common stock. Securities convertible into common stock consist primarily of debt securities or preferred stock which are exchangeable into a specified number of shares of common stock. On rare occasions, the Fund may purchase a warrant or a warrant and a non-convertible senior security in lieu of purchasing a conventional convertible security.

Investments will be made in a diversified list of securities with emphasis on those industries and companies which appear to offer the best means through which to realize the objective of long-term growth of capital. The Fund will select individual securities for investment after analyzing a company's business fundamentals to determine whether the current stock price represents good relative value in the marketplace. The Fund will also employ other quantitative methodologies to identify those securities that have reasonable prospects for superior relative price performance. The proportion of the Fund's assets invested in particular companies and industries will be changed from time to time depending upon management's evaluation of the outlook for specific industries and companies as well as for the economy in general.

The Fund intends to remain primarily, if not fully, invested in common stocks and securities convertible into common stock under normal market conditions. However, if market conditions necessitate a defensive posture, the Fund may temporarily invest all or part of its assets in fixed income securities including U.S. Government securities, corporate bonds (rated Baa or higher by Moody's Investors Service, Inc. or BBB or higher by Standard & Poor's Corporation), commercial paper (rated P-2 or higher by Moody's or A-2 or higher by S&P) and cash equivalents (such as bankers acceptances or certificates of deposit). The Fund may also invest in repurchase agreements which may involve additional risk. (See the Statement of Additional Information, Appendix, for further information regarding these types of investments.)

Prospective purchasers of shares of the Fund should recognize that there is no assurance that the Fund will meet its investment objective. Furthermore, the investment policies followed by the Fund will not eliminate the risk of loss inherent in the ownership of securities.

Investment Restrictions

The Fund has adopted several investment restrictions which may not be changed without shareholder approval. In addition to those restrictions set forth in the Statement of Additional Information, the Fund may not:

1. Make any purchase which would result in more than 5% of the value of its total assets being invested in the securities of any one issuer except United States Government securities.

2. Purchase the securities of any issuer if such purchase would result in more than 10% of the voting securities, or the securities of any class of such issuer, being held by the Fund.

3. Borrow money, except as a temporary measure for emergency purposes, in an aggregate amount exceeding 5% of the total assets of the Fund.

Figure 2-3. Spelling out the Investment Policies. Inside the prospectus, mutual funds must spell out the investment objectives and policies to which they refer briefly on the cover page, as well as investment restrictions which they have adopted. This example is from the prospectus of The Guardian Park Ave. Fund.

experience, control person, services to the fund, compensation paid by the fund), transfer agent, and dividend paying agent.

6. If applicable, a statement regarding brokerage commissions paid to any broker related to the fund's sponsoring organization, investment adviser, or main underwriter, or regarding any allocation of brokerage business that takes into account the sale of the fund's shares.

7. Description of the securities offered, including voting rights, any restrictions on retention or disposal, identification of those who control the fund prior to filing of registration statement, a statement regarding possible modification of rights by any means other than a majority vote of shareholders, identification of any other outstanding class of securities, and policy regarding dividends and distributions.

8. Description of how the shares being offered may be bought, including the names of any principal underwriter (and any relationship with the fund), a statement on how the offering price was determined, any sales charges that may be included, and any minimum initial or subsequent investment. If the fund directly or indirectly pays distribution expenses—which, therefore, are absorbed by shareholders—it also must describe them.

9. Explanation of procedures for redemption and any charges that may be imposed.

Statement of Additional Information. This statement is used to provide information not required, or supplementing that contained, in the prospectus. It may elaborate on investment objectives and policies, directors and officers (including any family relationships "not more remote than first cousin"), principal holders of securities, investment adviser(s), brokerage allocation and commissions, and underwriters and their commissions.

Other Reports. Funds are required to keep the SEC and shareholders up-to-date by submitting periodic reports to both. They must send reports quarterly to the SEC, but are obliged to send reports to shareholders only semiannually. (Many funds send shareholders quarterly reports, too.) In addition, they must send the SEC review copies of all promotional literature.

Semiannual reports must include a balance sheet and a statement of income (Figure 2-4), the amounts and values of the securities owned

STATEMENT OF ASSETS AND LIABILITIES

December 31, 1986

Assets

Investments at market (identified cost—$169,119,589)		$201,886,506
Cash		1,324
Receivable for:		
Securities sold	$7,345,975	
Shares of the Fund sold	1,426,326	
Dividends and interest	1,657,604	10,429,905
		212,317,735

Liabilities

Payable for:		
Securities purchased	7,583,953	
Shares of the Fund redeemed	130,460	
Capital gain distribution	1,122,929	8,837,342
Accrued expenses:		
Trustees' fees	4,000	
Management fees ..	1,044	
Other expenses ...	63,819	68,863
		8,906,205

Net Assets	$203,411,530
Shares of beneficial interest, no par value, outstanding	8,898,853
Net asset value per share*	$22.86

* Shares of the Trust are sold and redeemed at net asset value ($203,411,530 ÷ 8,898,853).

STATEMENT OF OPERATIONS

Year Ended December 31, 1986

Investment Income

Income	
Dividends	$ 4,024,005
Interest	3,721,612
	7,745,617
Expenses	
Management fee	929,075
Trustees' fees and expenses	14,394
Custodian	73,430
Transfer Agent	205,504
Audit	22,700
Legal	51,842
Printing	31,580
State excise tax	48,110
Insurance	22,566
Miscellaneous	2,355
	1,401,556
Net investment income	6,344,061

Realized and Unrealized Gain on Investments

Realized gain on investments	16,575,789
Unrealized appreciation	8,667,424
Net gain on investments	25,243,213
Net increase in net assets from operations	$31,587,274

Figure 2-4. Accounting for Assets and Income. Taken from an annual report of the Loomis-Sayles Mutual Fund, these statements show assets, liabilities, and the calculation of total net assets (left) and the increase in net assets resulting from the year's operations.

Statement of Investments
December 31, 1986

COMMON STOCKS (45.12%)

Shares		Cost	Value (Note 1)
	BROADCASTING (9.10%)		
235,500	Capital Cities/ABC, Inc.	$ 49,769,418	$ 63,143,438
	CONSUMER PRODUCTS (6.62%)		
2,000,000	Hasbro, Inc.	44,570,496	39,000,000
386,800	SSMC, Inc.†*	5,343,122	5,511,900
42,400	Sturm, Ruger & Company, Inc.	361,700	1,452,200
		50,275,318	45,964,100
	FOOD (10.65%)		
700,000	Kraft, Inc.	12,113,804	33,162,500
1,200,000	Sara Lee Corporation	14,915,388	40,800,000
		27,029,192	73,962,500
	INDUSTRIAL PRODUCTS (2.10%)		
540,200	Duplex Products, Inc.†	4,738,098	9,656,075
163,000	Kimball International, Inc. Class B.....................	4,458,000	4,930,750
		9,196,098	14,586,825
	PAPER MANUFACTURING (12.39%)		
745,500	Consolidated Papers, Inc...........................	22,645,750	38,486,437
1,949,400	P.H. Glatfelter Company†	12,726,070	47,516,625
		35,371,820	86,003,062
	PUBLISHING (.45%)		
48,000	Meredith Corporation	562,504	1,572,000
48,000	Meredith Corporation Class B.......................	562,504	1,572,000
		1,125,008	3,144,000
	RETAILING (2.23%)		
240,500	Melville Corporation	8,449,248	12,987,000
67,500	Weis Markets, Inc.	439,297	2,497,500
		8,888,545	15,484,500
	SERVICES (1.48%)		
324,500	PHH Group, Inc.	10,300,245	10,262,312
	Miscellaneous Securities **(.10%)**	715,575	713,400
	TOTAL COMMON STOCKS	$192,671,219	$313,264,137
WARRANTS (.21%)			
28,160	Capital Cities/ABC, Inc.	$ 941,600	$ 1,443,200

Principal Amount

U.S. GOVERNMENT OBLIGATIONS (54.67%)

$109,350,000	U.S. Treasury Bills due 3/26/87 through 8/6/87........	$106,713,076	$106,590,947
55,000,000	U.S. Treasury Notes, 9¾% due 4/30/87	55,052,094	55,635,938
55,000,000	U.S. Treasury Notes, 9⅛% due 5/31/87	55,054,489	55,635,938
91,000,000	U.S. Treasury Notes, 8½% due 6/30/87	91,242,923	92,080,625
69,000,000	U.S. Treasury Notes, 7⅛% due 3/31/88	69,062,873	69,668,437
	TOTAL U.S. GOVERNMENT OBLIGATIONS.........	$377,125,455	$379,611,885
	TOTAL INVESTMENTS (100%)‡	$570,738,274	$694,319,222

* Non-income producing
† Refer to Note 6
‡ The cost for federal income tax purposes is identical.

Figure 2-5. Telling Fund Shareholders What They Own. The statements of investments in fund annual reports tell shareholders what companies they have an interest in. This statement from Sequoia Fund's report is unusual not only for the low allocation of assets to stocks (45.12%) but also for the few (14) companies in which the fund held shares at the end of 1986.

(Figure 2-5), and a list of the purchases and sales of securities (other than government securities) during the period covered (Figure 2-6).

Requirements for annual reports are essentially the same with one major exception: The financial statements must be accompanied by a certificate stating that they were audited by independent public accountants.

Business Practices

Of the many regulations governing the business practices of mutual funds, the following areas are probably of greatest importance to you.

1. Restrictions on board of directors' membership. So-called "inside" directors cannot constitute more than 60% of a fund's board of directors. Funds that charge no sales commission, or "load," can have boards that include no more than one "outside" director.

2. Borrowing money and buying securities on margin.

3. The percentage of shares of another company which a fund can buy.

4. Changes in policies. No fundamental investment policies can be changed without a vote of the shareholders.

5. Relations with investment advisers. No investment adviser can serve a mutual fund without a written contract approved by a majority of shareholders. Among other things, the contract must prescribe compensation and cannot be for a term longer than two years.

6. Custody of funds' cash and securities. A fund must place its cash and securities in the custody of qualified commercial banks or brokerage firms that are members of a stock exchange.

7. Dividends. They can only be paid out of investment income.

8. Redemptions. Funds cannot suspend the right of redemption or postpone payment for more than seven days.

9. Sales load. It cannot exceed 8½%.

Six Months Ended October 31, 1986
($12,000,000 and above)

PURCHASES	Shares	Shares Owned October 31, 1986
Lincoln National Corp.	472,100	472,100
American Express Co.	401,100	401,100
British Petroleum Co. P.L.C.	625,400	625,400
Continental Corp. NY	507,900	507,900
Allied Signal Inc.	566,900	566,900
Amoco Corp.	333,600	333,600
Middle South Utilities, Inc.	1,003,200	1,489,500
Travelers Corp.	275,317	567,517
Chase Manhattan Corp.	322,520	623,906
Aetna Life & Casualty Co.	204,812	433,111

SALES	Shares	Shares Owned October 31, 1986
Borg Warner Corp.	578,200	—
Mobil Corporation	527,600	—
USX Corp.	887,300	—
Tenneco Inc.	350,000	—

Many of these investment changes were made over a period of time at different prices and conditions than now prevail. These transactions should be considered in connection with the policies of the Fund and the diversification of its investments and should not be regarded as a recommendation for similar action by other investors.

Figure 2-6. What Was Bought and Sold. Statements such as this one from the annual report of Vanguard's Windsor II list the principal changes in the fund's portfolio.

HOW FUNDS ARE ORGANIZED

Mutual funds may be a principal activity or a sideline for the management companies that sponsor them. The companies may regard the funds primarily as sources of profits, through the compensation received for serving as investment advisers, or as means of reinforcing other businesses or activities, such as securities brokerage and insurance.

Fund sponsors include not only firms in financial services—investment counselors, brokers, and insurance companies—but also associations (such as the American Association of Retired Persons and the American Medical Association), retail chains, and industrial companies.

An Example

A mutual fund's formation and operation bring into play a number of principals, some of whom may perform more than one function. To understand who does what, it's perhaps best to run through what happens when a fund is created.

As an example, we'll use one of the nearly 300 funds formed in 1986: Vanguard Quantitative Portfolios, Inc.*

Vanguard Group, Inc., which sponsors more than forty mutual funds, decided in early 1986 to start a new fund with a different investment objective: "To provide a total return (capital and income) greater than the total return of the aggregate U.S. stock market, as measured by the Standard & Poor's 500 Composite Stock Price Index."

Although the group is based in Valley Forge, Pennsylvania, the fund drew up articles of incorporation under Maryland law and filed them on April 8, 1986, then amended them in September. (To maintain an office in Valley Forge, it obtained permission to do business in Pennsylvania as a "foreign" corporation.) Allowing for ample growth, the papers provided for the issuance of up to one billion shares of common stock.

The Vanguard Group appointed Vanguard Quantitative Portfolios' first board, consisting of Vanguard Chairman John C. Bogle and eight outsiders. (As a no-load fund, it needed to name only one outsider.) They, in turn, appointed the fund officers who would manage its day-to-day operations: Bogle, as chairman, president, and chief executive officer; plus an executive vice-president, secretary, treasurer, and controller. In subsequent years, as in the case of other public cor-

---

*To illustrate these and other points throughout the book, we have, of course, used the names of actual funds. No citation is meant to imply endorsement.

porations, public shareholders would join insiders in voting for (or against) directors.

The board chose Franklin Portfolio Associates, Inc. of Boston, a subsidiary of Pittsburgh's Mellon Bank Corporation then advising 24 clients and managing assets exceeding $2 billion, to be the fund's investment adviser. (The Vanguard group acts as its own investment adviser for only a few of its funds; it turns to unaffiliated firms, such as Franklin, for all but one of its equity funds, the Vanguard Index Trust.)

The fund and Franklin signed an investment advisory agreement, effective November 1, 1986, and Franklin named John Nagorniak as portfolio manager and assigned a staff. The agreement stipulated that Franklin would manage the investment and reinvestment of the fund's assets, and select brokers and dealers to execute purchases and sales, all within the board's guidelines. Franklin would receive a basic annual management fee of .3% of the fund's average net assets for the first $100 million—or $300,000—plus or minus a certain percentage depending on how well or poorly the fund fared.

The fund's directors also chose Morgan Guaranty Trust Company of New York to be the custodian of the fund's portfolio of securities and cash, Price Waterhouse to be the auditors, and Vanguard Group itself to be transfer agent (to maintain shareholder records), dividend disbursing agent, and underwriter (to arrange for distribution of shares to the public). The board also agreed with the group that, for certain fees, the group would supply management, administrative, marketing, and distribution services, as well as office space and furnishings.

To provide the $100,000 minimum net worth required by the Investment Company Act before a fund can sell one share to the public, the Vanguard chairman, Bogle, bought 10,000 shares priced at $10 each. (The price was not mandatory; Vanguard could have issued 20,000 shares at $5. It chose $10 because 10 is an easier number to work with.) And the money was promptly put to work.

All of these steps having been taken, Vanguard was ready to bring in the public. On December 10, 1986, Vanguard Quantitative Portfolios filed a registration statement with the SEC. It had produced

50,000 copies of the prospectus and 2,000 of the statement of additional information, advertised the shares' availability in newspapers, sent promotional fliers to its existing funds' 1 million accounts, and was ready to accept requests.

Acting as its own distributor, Vanguard Group sold the shares to investors directly as well as indirectly through broker-dealers who, it advised in the prospectus, could charge a fee for their services.

By December 31, the fund had sold shares to 230 shareholders for $2.2 million and invested 88% in common stocks, led by IBM, Exxon, and the regional Bell Telephone companies. These investments and short-term assets generated enough interest and dividends so that, after deducting expenses, the fund could distribute a dividend of 3 cents per share in January.

Lifted by 1987's stock market surge and by Vanguard's aggressive marketing, the fund's total assets reached $25 million by the end of January—7 weeks after the public had bought the first shares—and $100 million by the end of March.

HOW FUNDS ARE CLASSIFIED

By Investment Objectives

All mutual funds are organized to achieve one of three investment objectives: capital gains, income, or a combination of the two. (Some also aspire to conserve capital—that is, to minimize or avoid capital losses. This is a noble, supplementary goal, to be sure, but insufficient to serve as a fund's *only* objective).

Funds differ in the degree to which they seek to attain their objectives, in the types and levels of risk they incur in the pursuit, in the mix of their portfolios, and, most important, in results. (They also differ in the taxability of income and/or capital gains distributions to their shareholders, but we won't dwell on these here.)

It is convenient to think of classes of funds in terms of the mere word or two that are thought to best convey their investment objectives. Therefore, these terms are widely used by periodicals, fund data services, and the funds themselves.

Investors are often confused, however, by the way in which these terms are applied by these sources—sources they want to rely on (see box below).

VARIETY IN OBJECTIVES

For a variety of reasons—including the desire of fund sponsors to sell more shares by differentiating their funds from others—they often express their investment objectives with considerable intricacy. While these statements of objectives can be boiled down to capital gains, income, or a combination of the two, they are modified or enveloped in wordy phrases so that it may be hard for investors to know what group a fund belongs in, what other funds it should be compared with, or possibly even what groups they should consider.

With new variants of investment objectives being continually introduced, due no doubt in part to fund marketers' competition for market shares, the number of funds has soared and investors' difficulties have been compounded. In the absence of an industry standard of terms to which everyone could adhere, each of the organizations that collect and disseminate mutual fund data has assigned funds to categories as it saw fit, and coined categories when it seemed necessary. The resulting confusion for anyone relying on more than one organization, which has led us to recommend that you look beyond the labels, becomes apparent as you look at various approaches.

INVESTMENT COMPANY INSTITUTE

All (member) mutual funds are divided into 11 categories* along the following lines:

Capital Gains

AGGRESSIVE GROWTH. Funds which seek maximum capital gains and essentially ignore current income. Aside from investing in common stocks of emerging or out-of-favor companies or industries, they may

*We're ignoring money market and tax-exempt funds here inasmuch as they generally *are* easy to classify.

---

also use specialized investment techniques such as option writing or engage in short-term trading.

GROWTH. Funds which also are more concerned with capital gains than income, but which are more inclined to invest in established companies and industries whose earnings are expected to continue to grow.

PRECIOUS METALS. Funds investing in the stocks of companies that mine gold and/or other precious metals.

INTERNATIONAL. Funds investing in stocks of foreign companies. Some of them, commonly referred to as global funds, may also invest in U.S. securities. (ICI published separate lists of international and global funds in its *Guide to Mutual Funds*, but has been combining the data for both groups in its annual *Mutual Fund Fact Book*.)

Income

INCOME. Funds that give the highest priority to generating maximum current income and try to achieve this goal by investing in dividend-paying common stocks and, occasionally, in corporate and/or government bonds.

OPTION/INCOME. Funds that seek high current return by investing primarily in dividend-paying common stocks on which call options are traded. Their current return generally consists of dividends, premiums from writing call options, gains from sales of securities on exercises of options, and any profits from closing purchase transactions.

U.S. GOVERNMENT INCOME. Funds that invest in a variety of government securities including Treasury bonds, federally guaranteed mortgage-backed securities, and other government issues.

GINNIE MAE. Funds that invest primarily in Government National Mortgage Association (Ginnie Mae) mortgage-backed securities.

CORPORATE BOND. Similar to income funds, these funds invest primarily in corporate bonds but also may buy the bonds of the U.S. Treasury or other government entities.

Capital Gains and Income

GROWTH AND INCOME. Funds investing mainly in the common stocks of established companies whose shares are expected to continue rising and paying dividends.

BALANCED. Funds that generally have three objectives—conserving principal, paying current income, and providing long-term growth of both principal and income—and try to realize them by owning a mixture of bonds, preferred stocks, and common stocks.

BARRON'S

Lipper Analytical Services, publisher of perhaps the most widely quoted fund performance data, which has been tracking funds since 1968, divides them into 20 categories, or nine more than ICI, all of which are used weekly in *Barron's* (and in its own reports). They differ from those of ICI in the following respects.

Capital Gains

GROWTH CATEGORIES. Lipper has three categories, instead of two, for funds with diversified portfolios: capital appreciation, for funds which ICI calls "aggressive growth," growth, and small company growth funds for those which limit investments to companies having a certain size.

INTERNATIONAL. Lipper has two categories: global funds, which invest 25% or more in securities traded outside the U.S. but which also may own U.S. securities, and international funds, which are totally invested in non-U.S. securities.

SECTOR. In recognition of the growth of sector funds, Lipper has established six categories. Five—health, natural resources, science and technology, "gold oriented," and utility—invest 65% or more in the indicated industries. The sixth, specialty funds, consists of funds which limit investments to any one of all the other industries.

OPTION GROWTH. Funds that seek to enhance capital gains by investing 5% or more in options.

Income

Lipper divides income-oriented funds into five categories which differ from ICI's five: fixed-income, which invest at least 75% in fixed-income securities (including preferred stocks as well as debt securities having short or long maturities); income, which seek high income by investing up to 75% in fixed-income securities and/or up to 60% in equities; option income; convertible securities; and world income.

Capital Gains, Preservation, and Income
Three fund categories constitute this group in Lipper's classification
system: equity income, funds which seek above-average and growing
income by investing at least 60% of their portfolios in common stocks;
growth and income, which look for growth of earnings and level or
rising dividends; and balanced, which try to attain their prime objective
of a stable net asset value by maintaining portfolios with an approximate
60–40 stocks-bonds balance.

AMERICAN ASSOCIATION OF INDIVIDUAL INVESTORS

It uses only seven categories: Four under capital gains (aggressive
growth, growth, precious metals, and international), one income category (bond), plus growth and income and balanced.

UNITED MUTUAL FUND SELECTOR

This newsletter uses 15 categories, including eight under capital gains
(similar to the foregoing but with the addition of natural resources),
three income, and three under capital gains and income (balanced,
equity income, growth and income).

CDA INVESTMENT TECHNOLOGIES, INC.

Seven categories: Four—aggressive growth, growth, international, and
metals—whose principal investment objective is capital gains; a bond
and preferred stock category for income, plus growth and income and
balanced.

FORBES

This magazine, which has published an annual survey since 1956, keeps
matters simple. It has only three categories: stock funds, balanced funds
(defined as funds in which stocks consistently make up 20 to 80% of
noncash assets), and bond and preferred stock funds.

DOW JONES-IRWIN

Dow Jones-Irwin's 1986 guide, *No-Load Mutual Funds,* divided stock
and bond funds into eight groups: Four primarily seeking growth (maximum capital gains, growth, emerging growth, and specialty), two pri-

marily seeking income (equity income and fixed-income), plus growth and income, and balanced.

BUSINESS WEEK

Data for this magazine, prepared by *Morningstar Inc.*, publisher of the *Mutual Fund Sourcebook* and *Mutual Fund Values*, are divided into 10 categories: Six seeking capital gains (maximum growth, growth, gold, international, small company, and specialty), two primarily seeking income (income and option/income) plus balanced and growth/income.

MONEY

The fund data of *Lipper Analytical Services*, which in mid-1987 replaced *Schabacker Investment Management* as this magazine's source, are presented in 15 groups—fewer than and slightly different from the groupings of Lipper data in Lipper's own publications and *Barron's:* Seven under capital gains (maximum capital gains, growth, international, global, small company growth, gold and precious metals, and sectors), six under income (equity income, option income, high yield corporate, high grade corporate, U.S. Government bonds and mort-gage-backed securities), and two under capital gains and income (growth and income, and balanced).

WIESENBERGER FINANCIAL SERVICES

This firm uses a more complicated method. It first divides funds by "primary objectives," of which it uses four (maximum capital gain, growth, income, stability) singly or in combinations in the order of priority (e.g., income and growth, growth and income). It then breaks these down by eight categories of "investment policy": Common stocks, balanced, bonds and preferred, bonds, Canadian and/or international, flexibly diversified ("usually, but not necessarily, balanced"), preferred stocks, and specialized (including insurance and bank stocks, public utility stocks, aviation and technology, and U.S. Government securi-ties).

This results in many combinations: Under maximum capital gain (common stocks), under growth (common stocks, specialized, Canadian and/or international), under income (bonds, bonds and preferred, flex-ibly diversified, specialized), under growth and income (flexibly di-versified, common stocks), under income and stability (common stocks, bonds, specialized, flexibly diversified) and under income/stability/ growth (balanced, bonds and preferred, common stocks).

With these 10 (and other) classification systems using different terms to categorize the same funds, it is easy to become confused. For illustration, look at Table 2-1 on the following page to see how five funds—Evergreen Total Return, Fidelity Magellan, Mutual Shares, Nicholas II, and Vanguard Wellesley Income are classified differently by the industry's trade association, mutual fund data services, and publications.

Under the circumstances, our advice to you is:

1. When considering a fund, check its prospectus to see how the fund itself states its investment objective.

2. Go to the financial statements in the prospectus and/or the most recent report to shareholders to determine its asset allocation and to see if the fund's investments are consistent with the stated objectives. If, for example, a fund claims to seek capital gains by investing in small companies, see how it defines "small," whether the definition seems right to you, and whether the companies in its portfolio fit the fund's own definition.

3. If you find it useful to study publications and data services to find funds whose investment objectives are of interest to you, be sure to understand how these sources define the categories.

To help you, we offer general definitions that may be helpful, by broad categories.

Capital Gains

Growth funds. Funds that invest in the common stocks of a diverse group of established, dividend-paying companies whose earnings— and, therefore, whose stock prices—are expected to grow as fast as, or faster than, the total of corporate profits. They may practice market

TABLE 2-1. Which Classification System Do You Use?

Fund	1	2	3	4	5	6	7	8	9	10
Evergreen Total Return	Bal	G&I	Bal	EI	S	G&I	EI	EI	G&I	I
Magellan	--	G	G	--	S	AG	G	G	AG	MCG
Mutual Shares	Bal	G	Bal	G&I	S	G&I	G&I	G&I	G&I	MCG
Nicholas II	G	SC	G	EG	S	--	SG	SC	G	G&I
Wellesley Income	Bal	Bal	Bal	FI	Bal	I	I	EI	I	I

Classification systems:

1 AAII
2 *Business Week*/Morningstar
3 CDA
4 Dow Jones-Irwin
5 *Forbes*
6 ICI
7 *Barron's*/Lipper
8 *Money*/Lipper
9 *UMFS*
10 Wiesenberger

Bal = balanced, G = growth, SC = small company, SG = small company growth, EG = emerging growth, G&I = growth and income, MCG = maximum capital gains, AG = aggressive growth, FI = fixed income, EI = Equity income, S = stock, I = income.

Note: Magellan did not appear in the AAII and DJ-1 no-load fund guides because it charges a 3% load. Nicholas II did not appear in the ICI directory because it is not an ICI member.

timing by allocating assets to cash when market prospects become doubtful and become fully invested in stocks when they expect higher stock prices. They may use options to hedge their positions. Funds investing in non-U.S. companies may expect not mere earnings growth in local currencies, but earnings growth after translation into U.S. dollars.

Aggressive growth funds. Funds that incur greater risks to try to maximize growth. They may buy the shares of a less well diversified group of less mature, growing companies which may only pay small dividends. They may be concentrated in the shares of a small number of companies. They generally stay almost fully invested in stocks, regardless of market conditions. They also may engage in speculative tactics: actively buying and selling options on stocks, borrowing money to buy more shares than their net cash inflow allows, or short selling.

Specialty (sector) funds. Funds that try to achieve faster growth by investing in a nondiversified group of companies. They may be firms in a single industry (loosely or narrowly defined), firms below a certain size, firms undergoing reorganization, firms that mine gold, and firms that operate within a specified geographical area (such as a state).

Income. The usual purpose of investing in income funds is, not surprisingly, the realization of income. When interest rates fall, income-oriented funds also can provide capital gains as their shares rise to reflect the increased values of their underlying securities. Income funds should not always be considered as vehicles for capital gains, however; when interest rates rise, as they did in Spring 1987, their shares fall and capital gains can turn into capital losses. Investors who had turned to income funds as a way of obtaining higher yields when money market rates declined, and who were not properly warned of the risks by the funds or by their brokers or other fund salespeople, learned this the hard way.

Taxable fixed-income. Funds that invest only in the nonconvertible debt securities (short- or long-term) and preferred stocks of corporations, in debt securities of the U.S. Treasury and government agencies, or in the fixed-income securities of both corporations and the government.

Tax-exempt income. Funds that invest in the debt securities of U.S. state and local governments, whose interest income is exempt from federal taxation and, depending on the securities, from state and local income taxes, too. Capital gains realized from the sale of these shares are subject to income taxes, however.

Capital Gains (and Preservation) and Income. Funds that are referred to as growth and income, balanced, equity-income, or total return fall into this group. They are the ones with the expressed aim of providing both capital gains and income—and sometimes capital preservation as well—but vary in the relative emphasis they accord each of these objectives.

To some two or more of these terms may be synonymous. To others they have different meanings. If a fund's sponsor wants the word "balanced" in its name, for example, the SEC requires the fund to maintain at least 25% of its assets in fixed-income senior securities. Yet a fund with a similar percentage of bonds may very well be called "growth and income."

What matters more to you than their names, you see, is what the funds own to enable them to offer you acceptable yields, relative price stability, and growth. Depending on their emphasis, their portfolios usually consist of common stocks plus various percentages of two or more of the following: Nonconvertible preferred stocks, nonconvertible bonds, convertible securities, and cash equivalents.

The common stocks are likely to be those of a diversified group of large companies, such as utilities, whose dividends are both reliable and high in relation to their share prices and whose earnings and dividends are expected to increase over time.

By Investment Strategies and Tactics

While we cannot cover all of the investment strategies and tactics employed by all fund managers, we can give you an overview. This background may help you to understand the differences in results as well as in goals and, thus, perhaps to choose among funds with similar attributes.

Asset Allocation. We have already commented considerably on asset allocation and will have more to say when we describe our strategy for fund selection. This is because we assign it a very high priority.

How much of a fund's net assets is invested in common stocks, fixed-income securities, and cash equivalents has a powerful influence on how well, or poorly, the fund performs.

An equity fund that is "fully" invested in stocks may be actually 97 to 99% in stocks, the rest being in cash equivalents to meet expected investors' requests for redemptions. If this is a fairly well fixed proportion, you don't need to know much more to be able to speculate how that fund will do in a bull market—as well as how it will fare in a bear market. In the latter case, it may be forced to liquidate securities that are otherwise worth holding if it doesn't have enough in cash to handle the predictable flurry of redemption requests.

An equity fund that has a deliberate policy of varying its allocation to stocks depending on market conditions will perform in a quite different way. In a bull market, it may be as much as 90 to 95% in stocks and do very well. If its portfolio manager is a good stock picker, it may outperform the market. Otherwise, it may lag the market a bit, but still satisfy its shareholders. By the time stock prices tumble, however, an astute—and perhaps also lucky—portfolio manager will have taken profits in stocks and gone into cash to the tune of 20% or more. This will enable the fund to ride out all but the worst slides in respectable shape. Naturally, if a fund went too greatly into cash too soon, its performance record would suffer in comparison with others.

Funds that invest in both equities and fixed-income securities fall into categories, too: those which have relatively constant allocations to each and those which vary allocations depending on market conditions. When both stocks and bonds do well, as was the case in much of the bull market that began in 1982, allocation between them is less important. If bonds are flat or slipping but stocks are rising, it will naturally be advantageous to be in funds that have a greater share of assets in stocks. If bonds are flat but stocks are expected to fall, a fund that's more heavily in bonds would be the choice.

Stock Selection. Few students of the market have given more sound advice than Will Rogers, who said something along the lines of: "Only buy stocks that's goin' up. If they ain't goin' up, don't buy 'em."

To comply with Will's counsel, portfolio managers of equity funds use what seems like an infinite variety of criteria—all in the hope of enhancing reward, moderating volatility, producing a reliable stream of current income, and so on.

The criteria they employ in looking for stocks they believe are "goin' up" include:

Price-earnings ratios below that of the S&P 500.

Current yields exceeding that of the S&P 500.

Only stocks that pay dividends.

Only stocks of companies that have been in business for X years.

Only stocks of companies that have not had a down year (or loss) in X years.

Only stocks of companies listed on the New York Stock Exchange.

Only stocks of companies whose profits have increased annually for X years.

Only stocks of companies whose sales revenue per share of common stock has gone up for X years.

Only stocks of companies that are "out of favor."

Only stocks of companies whose profits are sensitive to changes in interest rates.

"Large, well-known companies, but also smaller, less well-known companies which our Manager believes possess unusual values although they may involve greater risk."

"Companies which (the fund manager) believes have above-average growth characteristics . . . in the areas of earnings or gross sales which can be measured in either dollar or unit volume."

"Companies with valuable fixed assets."

"Securities that (the fund manager) believes are undervalued in relation to the issuing company's assets, earnings, or growth potential."

"Well positioned companies that may earn higher returns if conditions in their industry improve."

"Companies that have recently changed management or control and have the potential to experience sharply improved earnings."

"Securities of companies which are not closely followed" by institutional investors—presumably meaning, among others, all those competing equity fund portfolio managers.

Bond Selection. Compared to stock selection, bond selection seems to be a snap. All a portfolio manager has to be concerned with are credit risk, market risk, and inflation risk.

A fund essentially decides the degree of the risks it wishes to incur and articulates it for investors in terms of:

Concentration in U.S. Government securities. For those most concerned with safety, funds buy only bonds issued by the Treasury and other agencies of the government.

Credit ratings assigned by services such as Moody's Investors Service and Standard & Poor's. A fund placing emphasis on safety will go for bonds having no less than a specified grade—"investment grade" bonds, as they're called. One shooting for higher yield will drop down the grade ladder and pick bonds of corporations of lower credit worthiness.

Maturities. A fund serving institutions or others who can afford the risk inherent in them will choose long-term bonds. To incur even greater risk in hopes of higher returns, it may go for long-term bonds having lower credit ratings. For those who wish yields higher than money market rates but who don't wish to incur great market or inflation risks, funds buy bonds of shorter maturities.

Risk Control. To mitigate against unpredictable losses, funds may try to control risks by diversifying among maturities and by spreading corporate bond purchases among a large number of companies in a diverse group of industries. Thus a larger bond fund could offer less risk than a smaller one.

By Costs to Investors

When you begin to invest in mutual funds, you take a lot on faith, but there's one thing that should not remain vague: the costs you incur. At any time—but especially when you are considering a choice between two or more funds—you should know what it will cost you:

1. To get into the fund.
2. To stay in the fund.
3. To get out of the fund.

Costs of Entry. Perhaps the costs of mutual fund investing that are best known and most discussed are the sales commissions, or "loads." They are well known, in part, because funds that choose not to impose them have made the term "no-load" fund well known. They are discussed because some people contend they are unnecessary—that load funds perform no better than no-load funds—while others contend that investors receive advice or other services of value for the commissions they pay.

We lean to no-load funds for the reason just mentioned. We lean even more to the notion that you should know what costs you're incurring—and why—when you invest in mutual funds.

While the shares of more than 300 equity and bond funds are available without loads, those of many more funds involve sales charges of up to the limit of 8.5%. In the 1980s, a large number of funds—

new and existing—began to charge around 2–3%, giving rise to the term "low-load" funds.

Whatever the load, if you are considering a fund that involves one, you should know that *not one cent* of it is invested for you. If, for example, you put $1,000 into an 8.5% load fund, $915 is invested for you—no more. The remaining $85—which actually amounts to 9.3% of what's invested—goes to the broker who sold you the shares, the distributor, and/or others associated with the transaction, some of whom may be affiliated with the management company sponsoring the fund (Figure 2-7).

What you'd be doing is buying the number of shares to which $1,000 entitles you at the offering price. If prices didn't change and you'd

Sales Charge

The offering price to investors includes a sales charge, which is divided between the Distributor and the selling broker-dealer. The charge varies with the size of the purchase order but does not exceed 8¹/₂% of the offering price (equivalent to 9.29% of the amount invested). The sales charge varies as follows:

Amount of Purchase	Sales Charge		Dealer Discount as a Percentage of Offering Price
	As a Percentage of Offering Price	As a Percentage of Amount Invested	
Less than $10,000	8.50%	9.29%	8.00%
$10,000 but less than $25,000	7.50%	8.11%	7.10%
$25,000 but less than $50,000	6.00%	6.38%	5.70%
$50,000 but less than $100,000	4.00%	4.17%	3.80%
$100,000 but less than $250,000	3.00%	3.09%	2.85%
$250,000 but less than $500,000	2.00%	2.04%	1.90%
$500,000 but less than $1,000,000	1.00%	1.01%	0.95%
$1,000,000 or more	0.50%	0.50%	0.47%

In addition to the portion of the sales charge to be paid to dealers in accordance with the above schedule, the Distributor is offering an additional incentive to dealers until April 30, 1986. Dealers will be entitled to receive the full amount of all sales charges on sales of Company shares consummated prior to the close of business on that date. Persons who receive the Distributor's commission may be deemed to be underwriters within the meaning of the Securities Act of 1933.

Figure 2-7. An Example of How Load Fund Sales Charges Are Calculated. This typical sales charge table, which appears in the prospectus of National Aviation & Technology Corporation, shows how the load—expressed as both a percent of the offering price and of the amount invested—falls with the amount of a share purchase. The distributor of this fund is AFA Distributors, Inc., a wholly-owned subsidiary of its investment adviser, American Fund Advisors, Inc.

have to sell the next day, what you'd get back would be $915—based on the number of shares multiplied by the NAV. Your loss: $85.

If you had bought $1,000 worth of no-load fund shares at their NAV, the price didn't change, and you sold them the next day, you'd get back the $1,000.

While this is an unrealistic example, it serves to emphasize the difference between load and no-load funds.

Some funds go beyond imposing a load to provide an incentive to brokers who sell their shares. They also impose a load on shares bought when distributions are reinvested—shares that a broker had nothing to do with.

Costs of Staying in Funds. Once you own mutual fund shares, you are charged a variety of costs. One is of the sort you don't have to accept; the others are unavoidable, and your discretion is limited to choosing funds whose policies and practices will cost you less.

The fee you don't have to accept is the so-called 12b-1 fee, named for a 1980 SEC rule which permits a fund's assets to be used to pay its distribution costs. These charges, which cover items from preparation and distribution of sales literature and advertising to compensation of sales personnel, can run up to 1.25% of your assets annually; if you are planning to be in funds for a long term—the premise of our book—12b-1 fees could add up to significant sums.

But, as we said, you don't have to go into a fund that imposes it (or that reserves the right to impose it, as some say in their prospectuses that they do). There are many funds that don't charge it, and don't say they intend to, because the distribution and marketing costs are absorbed by the investment adviser or the fund management company.

The other costs are:

Investment management fee. This can run from 0.5% to 2.0% per year. It's based on the investment adviser's contract, spelled out in the prospectus. If the fund does well, there's no fee you'd rather pay. If the fund does very well, the adviser's contract may provide for a premium—just as it may provide for a penalty if the fund under-performs—and you'd not regret it.

The investment adviser's fee is not billed separately. It is included with the other expenses (next item) that are deducted from investment income to calculate net investment income.

Other expenses. These include custodial, legal, accounting, and transfer agent costs. They may run up to 1% or so of a fund's net assets per year.

A fund's financial statement, required by the 1940 Act, shows not only the total expenses per share but also the percentage of a fund's net assets that they constitute, as you saw in Figure 2-2. Together, the investment management fee and other expenses need not add up to more than 1.25%; you can find good funds that cost even less.

Brokerage costs. Funds have to pay brokers commissions when buying and selling securities. You hope to be in a fund that negotiates for the lowest commissions. You really never know whether it does, however, because brokerage costs are not itemized in a fund's financial statements; they're simply reflected in net asset value.

You *can* limit your exposure to high brokerage costs in one way though: by avoiding funds with high rates of portfolio turnover. Turn-over means transactions, and transactions mean brokers' commissions—whether high or low. A fund with a 100% portfolio turnover rate is a fund that turns over its entire portfolio in one year. Some exceed that by a wide margin. On the average, 60 to 70% turnover should be ample, and you can find fine funds with lower rates.

Income taxes. Funds' actions, beyond your control, can cost you more money than you might imagine. Funds have to distribute net investment income and proceeds from capital gains to their shareholders so that the funds themselves don't have to pay income taxes. When funds make such distributions, they are taxable income to you—whether you get cash or have the money reinvested in more shares.

A fund which frequently sells securities to realize capital gains has a high rate of capital gains distributions on which you must pay taxes.

Unless the securities sold would have dropped and the fund's capital gains would have evaporated, you would have been better off if the fund had deferred taking capital gains. Your shares would have had the same aggregate value as would have been the case if you had reinvested the distribution. But you would not have had to pay income taxes—yet.

Costs of Getting Out. The only cost of getting out of a mutual fund should be the income tax you pay on the gains you've realized (unless it's in an IRA, in which case the tax is deferred).

But some funds insist on getting something for themselves, too: a redemption fee. The fee can run up to 4% of the net asset value, a fairly steep cost—especially if the fund previously had charged a load to enter. A number of funds which impose it have a sliding scale, providing for a reduction each year the fund's shares are held.

There really is no need for you to get into a fund which charges a redemption fee, though (unless it's a fund that only imposes the fee for sales within a month or two of purchase to discourage frequent trading). Plenty of fine performers don't. To be certain whether it's imposed by a fund that you're considering, you have to look at the prospectus. It's not enough to look for the "r" (for redemption fee) in the mutual fund price tables in the newspapers; it's occasionally omitted.

HOW YOU DEAL WITH FUNDS

How You Get Information

To get a prospectus, recent periodic report, and any other information which a fund may have available, it is easiest to telephone—usually a toll-free 800 number—and make the requests. Some accept collect calls if they don't have 800 numbers. You'll find the numbers in the many newspaper and magazine advertisements or articles you see almost daily, in directories that may be available in your library, in ICI's $1 *Guide,* or in mutual fund newsletters. (A few even provide 24-hour phone service.) If you find it more convenient, you can clip the coupons contained in ads and mail them to the funds.

Once you get the materials you requested, you may find it necessary to telephone the funds with follow-up questions regarding anything that is unclear or omitted. During hours and days of heavy market activity, you may have trouble getting through and may have to be content with listening to canned music while you're "on hold." (Be grateful if it's good music.)

As a rule, you'll find the people on the telephone courteous and eager to help, but they are not always knowledgeable or able to be truly responsive. They may read from a script and be unable to go beyond the boilerplate.

If you are determined to get an answer that you can't get—an answer you believe you're entitled to—you may have to insist on speaking to some superior. This usually works. Sometimes, you may even be put through to the portfolio manager himself (herself).

How Fund Shares Are Sold

By definition, mutual funds are continuously offering new shares to investors, except for occasions when funds announce that they have suspended sales to new investors or to all (Tables 6-3 and 6-4).

Shares can be bought directly from the fund organizations—by mail, phone, or in person—and indirectly through full-service or discount brokerage firms, banks, financial planners, and life insurance companies, a number of which sponsor their own funds (Figure 2-8 illustrates how the fund industry is divided, on the basis of assets, between funds marketed directly and those marketed via sales forces.)

You simply fill out the proper form, mail or hand the fund or salesman a check for the amount you want to invest, and wait for a confirmation indicating how many shares you bought and at what price.

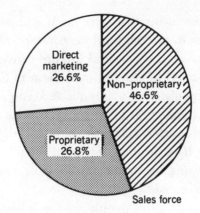

Figure 2-8. Mutual Fund Assets by Distribution Channel. Mutual funds whose shares are sold by sales forces—mostly those of broker-dealers, underwriters, and insurance companies—accounted for almost three-fourths of the $507 billion assets that all funds (including tax-exempts) had as of March 1987. Of these, funds *not* sponsored by the selling organization accounted for the larger share. Fund organizations which sell their own funds' shares directly to investors accounted for about one-fourth of the industry total. Their percentage has slipped in recent years with the boom in sales of government bond and GNMA funds, of which over 90% have been distributed via sales forces. Source: Investment Company Institute. Reprinted with permission.

If a lot of money is involved or if time is of the essence, you can have your bank wire the money via federal funds. Whatever you do, be sure to follow the fund's instructions, which are carefully spelled out in the prospectus.

Unless you specifically request one, you won't get a stock certificate. You really don't need it. Having the confirmation, followed by periodic statements, is sufficient proof that you own the shares and eliminates the need for safekeeping.

While some funds have none, most funds impose a minimum for an initial investment. They tend to run around $1,000; many are lower but others run as high as $25,000 or even higher. (For IRAs different minimums are likely to apply. See Chapter 8.) Additional investments usually can be made for $100 or even less.

How Fund Shares Are Redeemed

When an investor advises a fund, a fund's agent, or a broker-dealer by mail or telephone that he (she) wishes to sell shares, the fund or agent will mail a check or transfer money to the investor's bank account (unless the investor wishes to invest the proceeds in another fund sponsored by the same company), or pay the broker-dealer, who pays the investor. By law, the fund must redeem your shares within seven days. Fixed-income funds may offer investors checks which they can use to draw against their accounts. Anyone doing this must remember that each check results in a sale of shares that may, in turn, result in a taxable capital gain.

Prices at which Shares Are Bought and Sold

At the end of every day's market session, each fund (or agent) calculates the value of its assets and liabilities to determine its net assets. It next divides this figure by the number of shares then outstanding to compute the NAV per share.

For anyone investing in a "no-load" fund, the NAV is the purchase price. For anyone investing in load funds, the price is the offering price—that is, the NAV plus the "load."

When selling shares, all investors receive the NAV, but those reducing or eliminating their positions in funds that impose a redemption charge have it subtracted from the proceeds.

Mutual fund tables in the financial pages of newspapers tend usually contain three columns (Figure 2-9). The first lists the NAV for each fund. The second lists the offering price, if it's a load fund, or the letters "NL" if it's "no-load." The third column shows the change from the previous business day. Some papers, however, carry only the first two columns, forcing you to go to the previous edition to determine whether—and by how much—shares rose or fell.

MUTUAL FUND QUOTATIONS

Wednesday, July 1, 1987

Price ranges for investment companies, as quoted by the National Association of Securities Dealers. NAV stands for net asset value per share; the offering includes net asset value plus maximum sales charge, if any.

	NAV	Offer Price	NAV Chg.
Criterion Funds:			
Cm IncS	11.37	11.94-	.01
CvSecs	10.79	11.33-	.01
Globl Gr	13.84	14.53-	.04
Gov Inst	9.31	9.40-	.01
Inv Qual	9.49	9.96+	.01
Lowry M	10.22	10.73-	.01
Pilot Fd	11.93	12.52-	.02
Qlty TF	10.34	10.86+	.01
Sunblt G	22.67	23.80+	.01
US Govt	9.16	9.62	...
Cmbrind G	11.42	N.L.-	.04
Dean Witter:			
AmVal r	x14.60	N.L.-	.04
Cal TxFr	11.46	N.L.-	.02
Convrt r	12.23	N.L.-	.05
DevlGr r	10.21	N.L.+	.03
DivGro r	21.04	N.L.-	.07
G Plus	9.70	N.L.+	.01
High Yld	13.96	14.77-	.01
NatRes r	10.40	N.L.-	.03
NY TxFr	10.87	N.L.	...
Optionl r	9.78	N.L.-	.02
Sears Tx	10.95	N.L.-	.02
Tax Adv	10.21	N.L.-	.02
Tax Ex	10.76	11.21	...
USGovt r	9.96	N.L.-	.01
WWIT r	17.36	N.L.+	.03
Delaware Group:			
Dectr I	20.19	22.07-	.05
Dectr II	11.95	12.55-	.03
Del Cap	14.21	14.92-	.01
Delchs F	8.04	8.62	...
DTR Inv	9.87	N.L.	...
GNMA	8.88	9.32+	.01
US Govt	8.67	9.10	...
TxFr Pa	7.61	7.99	...
TFr USA	10.93	11.48+	.01
TF USAI	10.32	10.83+	.01
Delw Fd	22.26	24.33-	.05
Delta Td	9.07	9.91-	.05
Destiny I	15.90	(z) -	.03
Destiny II	20.97	(z) -	.01
D.I.T.			
Cap Gr	16.19	N.L.+	.06
Cur In	10.14	N.L.	...
Gov Sec	9.98	N.L.+	.01
OTC Gr	30.42	N.L.-	.02
DFA Fxln	101.31	N.L.+	.03
DFA Small	10.43	N.L.	...
D G DvSrs	27.76	N.L.	...
DodgC Bal	37.55	N.L.-	.07
DodgC Stk	40.07	N.L.-	.11
DbEx Cap	10.24	10.48	...
DbEx Flx	11.43	11.91	...
Drexel Burnham:			
DB Fund	24.37	25.25-	.06
DSTGv r	xd9.69	N.L.-	.11
DSTOp r	xd10.62	N.L.-	.27
DST Cv r	xd10.38	N.L.-	.22
DSTBd r	x10.93	N.L.-	.07
DST Gr r	x14.30	N.L.-	.08
DST E r	15.63	N.L.-	.02
Fenint r	14.47	N.L.+	.03
TxFr Ltd	10.54	10.70	...
TF Long	9.62	10.05+	.01
Dreyfus Group:			
A Bonds	13.86	N.L.-	.09
CalT Ex	14.60	N.L.+	.02
Cap Val	23.57	24.68+	.01
Cnv Sec	9.32	N.L.-	.04
Dreyf Fd	13.95	15.25-	.02
Dreyf Lv	20.21	22.09-	.18
GNMA	x14.94	N.L.-	.11
Growth	12.15	N.L.+	.03
Insr TE	17.26	N.L.+	.02
Intrmd	13.65	N.L.+	.02
Mass Tx	15.65	N.L.+	.02
New Ldr	25.19	N.L.-	.11
NYT Ex	14.95	N.L.+	.05
Str Inc	13.28	13.69	...
Str Inv	17.13	17.66-	.13
Tax ExB	12.20	N.L.+	.01
Third Cn	7.96	N.L.+	.07
Eaton Vance Funds:			
Cal Mn r	10.02	N.L.-	.01
EH Stk	x14.84	16.00-	.16
Gov Obli	(z)	(z)	...
Growth	8.79	9.23	...
Hi Inc r	9.88	N.L.	...
Hi Mun r	9.70	N.L.	...
High Yld	x5.14	5.40-	.15
Inc Bost	10.19	10.70-	.01
Invests	8.41	8.83-	.01
Muni Bd	x8.74	9.18-	.05
Naut Fd	d13.24	13.90-	1.04
Spc Eqty	d18.95	20.43-	.08
Tot Ret	x10.07	10.57-	.21
VS Specl	xd12.41	13.03-	.15
Eclipse Eq	10.11	N.L.	...
Empir Bld	16.51	17.33	...

	NAV	Offer Price	NAV Chg.
Flex Funds:			
Bond	(z)	(z)	...
Growth	(z)	(z)	...
Inc Gr	(z)	(z)	...
Retire	(z)	(z)	...
Fortress Investment:			
Conv Inc	10.04	N.L.	...
GISI	9.46	9.56+	.01
HI Qual	13.33	N.L.+	.02
44 Wall St	3.76	N.L.-	.05
44 WS Eqt	7.15	7.22-	.06
Founders Group Funds:			
Frontr	12.51	N.L.	...
Growth	10.69	N.L.-	.02
Income	16.83	N.L.-	.05
Mutual	9.45	N.L.-	.04
Special	35.02	N.L.-	.06
FPA Funds:			
Capital	13.46	14.40-	.04
New Inc	9.39	9.83	...
Paramt	15.59	16.67-	.09
Perenni	19.55	20.91-	.01
Franklin Group:			
AGE Fd	x3.55	3.70-	.04
Cal Ins	10.66	11.10+	.02
Cal TxFr	x6.80	7.08-	.04
Corp Csh	9.15	N.L.+	.03
D N T C	13.02	13.56-	.03
Equity	7.69	8.01-	.04
Fed TxF	x10.98	11.44-	.07
Gold Fnd	14.16	14.75+	.07
Growth	19.66	20.48-	.04
Income	2.30	2.40	...
Ins TxFr	10.87	11.32	...
Mass TF	10.32	10.75+	.01
MN Ins	10.90	11.35	...
N Y Tax	x10.78	11.23-	.07
OHIn TF	10.60	11.04+	.01
Optn Fd	xd6.07	6.32-	.25
Mich TF	10.58	11.02+	.01
Puer TF	10.49	10.93	...
US GvSc	x7.10	7.40-	.05
Utilities	7.93	8.26+	.01
Freedom Funds:			
EqVal r	10.30	N.L.-	.02
Global	(z)	(z)	...
GI IncPI	10.67	N.L.+	.01
GldGv r	15.47	N.L.+	.03
GvPlus r	9.80	N.L.+	.02
RegBk r	12.29	N.L.+	.03
FundTrust:			
Aggr f	15.50	N.L.-	.10
Grow f	14.99	N.L.-	.12
Gro Inc f	14.14	N.L.-	.09
HY Inv	10.05	10.47	...
Incom f	10.45	N.L.+	.01
GabelliA	13.92	N.L.-	.01
Gatewy Gr	11.89	N.L.+	.01
Gatewy Op	15.69	N.L.-	.04
Geico ARP	25.27	N.L.+	.01
GenAgg G	24.16	N.L.-	.16
Genl Elec Invest:			
Elf TxE	10.67	N.L.-	.02
Elfn Inc	10.80	N.L.	...
Elfn Tr	32.30	N.L.	...
S&S LT	11.21	N.L.	...
S&S Pro	41.16	N.L.-	.03
GenlSec r	12.01	N.L.-	.01
Genl TxEx	13.37	N.L.+	.02
Gintel Group:			
Cap App	12.03	N.L.-	.07
Erisa	43.43	N.L.-	.26
Gintl Fd	66.66	N.L.-	.46
Govaars	10.50	N.L.	...
Grad EstG	17.49	N.L.-	.03
Grad Opp	13.27	N.L.+	.01
GIT Investment:			
Eq Spec	(z)	(z)	...
IncA Rt	(z)	(z)	...
Income	(z)	(z)	...
TxFr HY	(z)	(z)	...
Granit Gr	18.31	N.L.+	.02
Grth IndSh	11.04	N.L.	...
GrF Wash	12.91	13.59-	.09
GT Global:			
Europe	(z)	(z)	...
Intl	21.68	22.77+	.17
Japan	22.78	23.91-	.58
Pacific	25.36	26.62-	.34
Guardian Funds:			
Bond	11.48	N.L.+	.01
Park Av	24.67	26.96-	.02
Stock	20.30	N.L.-	.04
Harbor G	13.03	N.L.-	.05

	NAV	Offer Price	NAV Chg.
Liberty Family Fds:			
Am Lead	14.34	15.02+	.01
HI Incm	12.11	12.68+	.01
Tax Free	10.11	10.59+	.02
US Gvt S	8.44	8.84	...
Lib MutG	x9.79	10.20-	.07
Ltd Term	12.68	13.04-	.01
LndnrDv r	23.12	N.L.-	.05
LindnrFd r	19.14	N.L.	...
LMH Fund	25.50	N.L.+	.01
Loomis Sayles Funds:			
Cap Dev	28.02	N.L.+	.19
Mutual	27.09	N.L.-	.02
Lord Abbett:			
Affiliatd	12.54	13.52-	.04
Bnd Deb	10.41	11.22-	.01
Devl Gro	9.59	10.34+	.03
Fd Valu	11.25	12.13-	.06
Govt S	3.05	3.20-	.01
TxFr Cal	9.93	10.43+	.02
TxF Natl	10.41	10.93+	.02
TxFr NY	10.58	11.11+	.01
Value Ap	11.99	12.93-	.01
Lutheran Brotherhood:			
Broth Fd	19.53	20.56	...
Bro HY	x10.16	10.69-	.09
Bro Inc	x8.54	8.99-	.08
Bro MBd	7.93	8.35	...
MacKay Shields:			
CapAp r	12.20	N.L.	...
Conv r	10.10	N.L.-	.01
CorpB r	9.49	N.L.	...
GovtP r	9.54	N.L.	...
TF Bd r	9.71	N.L.+	.01
Value r	10.75	N.L.-	.04
Mathers	18.81	N.L.+	.01
Meeschr C	30.37	N.L.-	.22
Merit PA	11.70	N.L.+	.03
Merrill Lynch:			
Basc Val	20.21	21.61-	.05
CalTxE r	10.97	N.L.+	.02
Captl Fd	24.43	26.13-	.06
Corp Dv	10.90	11.12	...
EqBd 1 r	14.07	14.66-	.01
EuroF r	11.09	N.L.+	.02
Fed Sec	9.43	10.06	...
Fd FT r	17.26	N.L.-	.07
Hi Incm	8.41	8.76+	.01
Hi QualP	11.28	11.75	...
Inst Int	9.66	N.L.	...
Intl Hldg	14.41	15.41+	.03
Inter TP	11.25	11.48	...
Muni Ins	7.78	8.10-	.01
Mun HY	10.12	10.54	...
NY Mn r	10.66	N.L.+	.01
Ltd Mat	9.82	9.89-	.01
Munil r	9.50	N.L.+	.03
NatRes r	17.68	N.L.+	.02
Pacific	41.76	44.66-	.19
Phoenx	14.29	15.28	...
RetBn r	12.16	N.L.-	.01
RetEq r	10.08	N.L.-	.01
RetInc r	9.54	N.L.+	.01
RetGIB r	10.57	N.L.-	.02
Sci Tech	12.20	13.05-	.02
Sp'l Valu	14.58	15.59-	.06
MetLife State Street:			
Cap App	11.87	12.43+	.01
Eq Inc	10.34	10.83-	.01
Eq Invs	11.30	11.83-	.03
Gvt Inc	11.96	N.L.+	.01
HI Inc	7.49	7.84+	.01
Tax Ex	7.03	7.36-	.01
MFS:			
MIT	15.28	16.47-	.07
Finl Dev	13.85	14.93-	.04
Grth Stk	11.94	12.87-	.04
Cap Dev	13.86	14.94-	.05
TxFr CA	x4.94	5.19-	.01
Special	9.94	10.72-	.05
Sectors	12.55	13.18-	.06
Emg Gr	20.77	22.39-	.08
Gv Guar	x9.68	10.16-	.06
Intl Bd	12.05	12.99-	.36
Gov HiY	xd8.88	9.32-	.08
TxF MD	x10.37	10.89-	.07
Finl Bd	x13.22	14.25-	.09
HiInc Bd	x6.81	7.34-	.06
Muni Bd	x10.18	10.69-	.06
Muni HY	x9.80	10.29-	.07
TxEx SC	x10.96	11.51-	.07
TxFr NC	x10.94	11.49-	.05
TxFr VA	x10.59	11.12-	.08
TxF MA	x10.44	10.96-	.06

	NAV	Offer Price	NAV Chg.
Piper Jaffray:			
Balanc	9.78	10.19-	.02
GovInc	9.66	10.06+	.01
SectP	10.01	10.43-	.01
Value	10.29	10.72-	.03
Plym IGr	10.97	11.31	...
Plym Spc	18.44	19.01+	.01
Price Rowe:			
Cal TxF	9.25	N.L.-	.01
Cap Apr	11.61	N.L.-	.04
Eqty In	14.39	N.L.+	.01
GNMA	9.71	N.L.	...
Growth	19.71	N.L.-	.07
Grw Inc	14.53	N.L.-	.03
High Yld	10.74	N.L.+	.01
Income	8.65	N.L.	...
Intl Bd	10.32	N.L.	...
Intl Stk	30.36	N.L.-	.12
MD TxF	9.11	N.L.-	.02
New Am	14.55	N.L.+	.01
New Era	21.88	N.L.-	.07
Nw Horz	14.48	N.L.-	.03
NY TxFr	9.41	N.L.	...
S-T Bond	5.08	N.L.+	.01
TxFr Inc	8.81	N.L.	...
TxFr HY	11.12	N.L.-	.01
TxFr SI	5.13	5.14-	.01
Primry T	11.61	N.L.-	.01
Principal Preserv:			
Div Ach	10.43	10.92-	.05
Hedg TE	8.58	8.98+	.01
Insr TE	9.15	9.58+	.01
S&P 100	13.01	13.62-	.03
GOVT PI	9.38	9.82	...
Princor Funds:			
Cap Ac	21.54	23.55-	.12
GSIF	x10.34	10.88-	.06
Growth	23.13	25.28-	.14
Prudential Bache:			
Adjust R	23.14	N.L.	...
CalMn r	10.78	N.L.-	.01
Equity r	x10.90	N.L.-	.09
EqInc r	10.36	10.68-	.04
Global r	12.26	N.L.-	.01
GMNA r	15.15	N.L.+	.02
GovtPl r	9.95	N.L.+	.01
GvP II r	9.35	9.64+	.02
Govt Sec	10.37	N.L.+	.02
Grwth r	13.86	N.L.-	.02
HiYld r	10.55	N.L.	...
InVer r	11.88	N.L.-	.03
MnNY r	10.79	N.L.	...
MuniAz r	10.80	N.L.-	.02
MunGA r	10.93	N.L.-	.02
MunMa r	10.56	N.L.-	.01
MnMD r	10.19	N.L.-	.02
MunMi r	10.86	N.L.+	.01
MnMN r	11.00	N.L.	...
MunNC r	10.57	N.L.+	.01
MunOh r	10.87	N.L.-	.01
MunOR r	10.67	N.L.-	.02
MunPA r	9.76	N.L.	...
NtlMun r	15.13	N.L.-	.02
OptnGr r	9.31	N.L.-	.03
Resrch r	14.96	N.L.-	.07
Util Fd r	14.31	N.L.-	.03
Putnam Funds:			
CCT Arp	46.17	47.35	...
CCT Dsp	46.81	48.01	...
Cal TxE	15.04	15.79+	.02
Captl Fd	8.89	N.L.-	.03
Convert	17.66	19.30-	.03
Enrgy R	14.60	15.96-	.04
George	14.72	16.09-	.05
Gnma PI	10.47	10.99+	.01
Gro Inc	13.98	15.28-	.02
Hlth Sci	22.48	24.57-	.09
Hi Incom	11.37	12.19+	.02
High Yld	15.46	16.58+	.01
H Yld II	11.56	12.40+	.01
Income	6.98	7.49	...
Info Sci	19.22	21.01-	.04
Intl Equi	32.60	35.63-	.07
Investr	10.25	11.20-	.03
MATx r	11.74	N.L.+	.01
MI Tax r	11.86	N.L.+	.02
MNTx r	11.70	N.L.+	.01
OHTx r	11.67	N.L.+	.02
NY TEx	16.33	17.14+	.02
Option	11.62	12.70-	.02
Option II	11.39	12.45-	.08
OTC Em	30.42	32.62-	.02
Tax Ex	24.37	25.59+	.03
TF HY r	13.71	N.L.+	.01
TF In r	13.77	N.L.+	.03
US GGtd	14.26	14.97+	.02
Vista Bs	21.72	23.74-	.10
Voyage	25.08	27.41+	.03
Quasar As	68.60	N.L.+	.09
Quest for	28.17	N.L.-	.05
Rainbw Fd	xd5.73	N.L.-	.79
ReaGra Fd	14.34	15.67+	.01
ResEqCn f	18.95	N.L.	...
Rch &Teng	16.98	N.L.-	.05

Figure 2-9. Mutual Fund Quotations. An excerpt from *The Wall Street Journal*'s daily table of mutual fund net asset values and NAV changes. Reprinted by permission of *The Wall Street Journal*, © Dow Jones & Co., Inc. 1987. All rights reserved.

If a fund imposes a redemption charge, the newspapers carry the letter "r" to indicate it (or should). When a dividend or capital gains distribution has been declared, payable to all who held a fund's shares on that day—the "day of record"—the NAV is reduced by the amount and an "x" is inserted next to the NAV to indicate the shares are trading "ex-dividend" or a "d" to indicate they're trading "ex-distribution."

After the market's close every afternoon, the prices and changes for all funds—that is, all that have 1,000 shareholders or $25 million in assets—are fed by the funds or their agents into the computers of the National Association of Securities Dealers Automated Quotations system (NASDAQ). This is the same system which collects and disseminates over-the-counter securities prices.

About 5:30 P.M., NASDAQ, in turn, transmits all the data electronically to *The Wall Street Journal* and to the Associated Press and United Press International for resending to other newspapers. Any fund that misses the deadline is rewarded the next morning by having a "z"—for "not available"—next to its name, instead of the new NAV, in newspapers from coast to coast.

Convenience of Transactions

Although there may be exceptions among funds, no other means of investment compares with mutual funds in the convenience afforded an average individual when initiating purchases, adding to one's position, changing investment strategy, or selling shares.

A prospectus, supplementary information about a fund, and an application form are easily obtained by mail, telephone, or in person. Between statements, balances can be checked by phone, too.

Initial and additional investments, which usually can be made in modest amounts, are commonly paid for by check, but many funds make it possible for investors to transfer money directly from their banks to the funds' bank accounts.

Sales of shares can be arranged by telephone or mail just as easily, and the proceeds can be transmitted by check or deposited directly

to investors' bank accounts. Automatic withdrawals of distributions
can also be arranged.

Easy as it is to get out of one fund and into another, it is even
easier when one switches among funds within a fund family. A single
telephone call can do the job. The simplicity may tend to make one
forget the possible tax consequences of switching; unless the account
is an IRA or other tax-sheltered account, income tax will be due on
any capital gains.

Ease of Record Keeping

To help you keep track of your investments and fill out income tax
returns properly, funds send you confirmations following every transaction and periodic statements. At the end of the year, they send out
cumulative statements that list all of the year's purchases and redemptions—including the numbers of shares and dollars involved in
each case—and all income and capital gains distributions. In addition,
funds send you a copy of a form they send to the Internal Revenue
Service which aggregates all of your taxable items to enable IRS to
check your return.

While you may wish or need to do record keeping of your own,
you will find the fund's statements very useful. For both investment
management and tax reasons, you should retain the fund's statements
for several years.

3

THE CHECKERED HISTORY OF THE MUTUAL FUND INDUSTRY

Although many of the mutual funds we know today are of relatively recent origin, their fundamental role—to serve as a vehicle for the pooling of investors' money and for the diversification of investments to reduce risk—can be traced back well over 150 years. King William I of the Netherlands has been credited by some with founding the first investment company in 1822; before long, the idea had spread to the United Kingdom and the United States.

The common purpose of the earliest companies, as valid today as when expressed by Britain's Foreign and Colonial Government Trust at its establishment in 1868, was to provide "the investor of moderate means the same advantages as the large capitalists in diminishing the risk of investing . . . by spreading the investment over a number of different stocks."

THE INVESTMENT COMPANY CONCEPT

As public purchases of the securities of U.S. industrial companies and railroads increased during the economic boom that followed the Civil War, the investment company concept became attractive to many American investors.

Whether called investment trusts, investment companies, or something similar, and whether formed by bankers, stockbrokers, or investment counseling firms, they had one common objective: to earn income by investing in the common stocks and other securities of business corporations. They were not, however, to operate the businesses of, or to exercise control over, the corporations in which they invested. All fell primarily into two categories:

> Management companies—organized as corporations or business trusts—which sold shares to investors, bought the securities of business corporations with the money, and managed their portfolios (i.e., they sold when holdings became unattractive, and reinvested the proceeds in others that held greater promise).
>
> Unit investment trusts, which sold to investors shares representing fractional interests in fixed numbers of securities in specified corporations, but made little or no effort to manage their portfolios.

Once established, with fixed numbers of their own securities authorized and outstanding, management companies did not sell additional shares to the public or buy them back. Anyone wishing to own shares of such a company had to buy them from someone else, as if making an ordinary stock purchase. And, as was (and remains) the case with ordinary transactions, the price of a particular share reflected its supply–demand balance at that moment. It could equal, exceed, or fall short of the share's interest in the current aggregate market value of the management company's portfolio. Such companies, still popular with many, became known as closed-end management investment companies, or simply closed-end funds.

THE FIRST MUTUAL FUND

Formation of the nation's first open-end management investment company, or mutual fund, followed in 1924, when Massachusetts Investors Trust was established. The idea of a fund which would continuously sell and redeem its shares—at a price equal to the net per-share value of its assets—apparently occurred at about the same time to a number of Bostonians.

Working both in small groups and alone, they hit upon the notion while considering new investment vehicles to accommodate (or exploit) public demand for stocks during the booming market of the Roaring Twenties.

One group consisted of two stockbrokers and a lawyer "who were fairly well informed on conventional trusts as managed by banks and individual trustees and who began to see ways of cross-pollinating the trust and securities fields," according to MIT's history. Another consisted of three well-to-do young commercial and investment bankers who decided to pool their own funds to buy common stocks in a joint investment account with the understanding that any of them could withdraw his share at the current market value. There was also a young salesman who, after selling shoes, books, and pots and pans, was selling investment trust shares for an investment firm and wanted to adopt the mutual savings bank practice of allowing depositors to withdraw their money whenever they wanted.

It was not long before others joined MIT. As its organization papers were being drawn up, State Street Investment Corporation was being created a few blocks away. Begun as an investment vehicle for the founders and their friends, it did not offer its shares to the public until 1927. The year 1928 saw the birth of five other mutual funds still active today—Century Shares Trust, Industrial and Power Securities Company (known since 1935 as the Wellington Fund), National Aviation & Technology Corp., Pioneer Fund, and Scudder, Stevens & Clark Balanced Fund (known since 1977 as Scudder Income Fund). By year's end, total assets of all mutual funds had passed $100 million.

The growth in the number and assets of mutual funds was not really impressive, however, when compared to the explosion in closed-end funds. Their birth rate had accelerated from about 20 per year in the early 1920s to over 100 by 1927. Heavily promoted in sales literature that made extravagant—not to say unjustified—claims, they appealed to a public expecting overnight riches during this period of euphoria. With stock prices soaring, closed-end fund prices could, and did, soar even more as the premiums over the market values of their underlying securities increased. Nothing illustrated this better than the share offering of Goldman Sachs Trading Corporation, the largest of its type, which raised $330 million between December 1928 and the summer of 1929. In the first three months of the offering, the fund's shares more than doubled, while stock price averages only rose 10% or so.

THE CRASH AND ITS EFFECTS

It was too good to last. After eight years in which the S&P index had risen almost fivefold, the bull market peaked in September. Drifting lower at first, stock prices began to collapse in the "crash" of late October. By the time the bear market ended nearly three years later, the index had fallen 86%.

As share prices tumbled, institutional investors such as mutual and closed-end funds—with all their professional skills—suffered losses along with individual investors. Of the two types of investment companies, closed-end funds, however, suffered far more. Many failed altogether.

For one thing, the share prices of closed-end funds fell more steeply than those of mutual funds because of the basic difference in the way their share prices are established. Having soared, for example, to 200% of underlying market values—that is, to a 100% premium—when the market rose, a closed-end fund's share price could fall 75%—to 50% of market values, or a 50% discount—when the market slumped. Mutual fund shares, in comparison, only fell as much as the values of their underlying assets—which was bad enough, but not as bad.

Another reason that prices of a number of closed-end fund shares dropped more severely was that they had taken excessive risks. Instead of merely investing the cash they had raised by selling shares, their promoters also had borrowed money to buy more stocks. Thus, when their investments soured and they had to sell assets to pay off loans, little or nothing was left for the funds' shareholders.

The small number of more conservatively managed mutual funds were better able to survive, but it wasn't easy. Like the closed-end funds that remained afloat, they had to judge which stocks to unload and which, if any, to buy at the bargain prices then prevailing. Like the surviving closed-end funds, they also had to try to maintain dividend payments to their shareholders. But unlike the closed-end funds, the mutual funds faced an additional challenge: to manage their cash and other assets well enough to be able to accommodate shareholders who wanted to redeem their shares. A couple of the mutual funds had a slightly easier time than the others. Having invested in bonds as well as stocks—thereby becoming the models for what since became known as balanced funds—their total asset values held up better than the rest.

The decline in asset values and share redemptions combined to slash mutual funds' total assets by over 50% in two years—from $134 million at the end of 1929 to $64 million at the end of 1931. It was from this base that the industry's growth soon began anew.

RECOVERY

With closed-end funds devastated and the public's appetite for new closed-end fund shares negligible at best, mutual funds emerged as an attractive alternative for investors eager to participate in the stock market's recovery.

While existing funds picked up momentum, new ones were being conceived. Among them were the first funds of the Fidelity, Seligman, Eaton Vance, Calvin Bullock, Axe-Houghton, Safeco, and Lord, Abbett groups and, in perhaps the most ambitious undertaking of 1932, the newly-incorporated Keystone organization launched four stock and four bond funds. Differentiated according to levels of risk exposure, the eight constituted the first fund family. Other sponsors were subsequently inspired to form new funds as stocks roared back from their 1932 bottom. By the end of 1936, total mutual fund assets had grown beyond $500 million.

With the strong demand for stocks and the accelerated rate of mutual fund formation came unsavory management practices which threatened public confidence in the funds, as they undermined trust in stocks generally. Among brokers, securities dealers, investment bankers, and commercial bankers who were in position to dominate the boards and control the managements of funds were some unscrupulous operators who advanced the interests of their other businesses at the expense of funds they had organized. Share prices, while based on net asset values, were set by some in a way that permitted insiders to redeem their holdings on a more favorable basis. In certain cases, dividends declared and paid constituted a return of capital, not the expected distribution of investment income, but shareholders were not advised. Investment policies were sometimes changed and some managements gave themselves long-term contracts without the consent, or even the knowledge, of shareholders.

Shareholders usually could do nothing about these or other practices when they discovered them because, as they learned too late, fund managements and distributors had been issued shares with special voting rights which gave them a greater voice in running the funds.

It had become increasingly clear that the mutual fund industry needed reforms that would eliminate abuse of the public—and, indeed, preserve the industry. The government, however, had first to turn its attention to the even more widespread dishonesty and deceit which affected the ownership of, and transactions in, corporate securities generally.

THE INTRODUCTION OF REGULATION

The government's first move was to introduce a set of regulations aimed at reducing, if not eliminating, the risk that investors could be led into buying worthless securities through misrepresentation. It did this by approving the Securities Act of 1933, whose principal objective was to require fair and full disclosure of material facts regarding securities offered or sold in interstate commerce. Disclosure was to be achieved by filing detailed registration statements covering new shares with the Federal Trade Commission and the submission of prospectuses, containing the most important information, to prospective purchasers.

The government's next step, the Securities Exchange Act of 1934, which created the Securities and Exchange Commission to replace the FTC as the securities policeman, expanded information requirements by mandating periodic corporate reports to keep shareholders up-to-date.

In dealing with corporate securities generally and in focusing on the dissemination of information as the principal remedy for abuses, both acts failed to address facets of investment companies which gave unscrupulous promoters unique opportunities for imprudent or unethical practices. Moreover, a large number of investment companies were not covered by either act.

Demands for investment company reform led Congress in 1935 to ask the newborn SEC to study the functions and activities of investment trusts and companies, including their policies and influence, and report back. Congress' objective: additional legislation to help to ensure that the public would no longer be exploited by any open- or closed-end funds.

During the course of extensive hearings, discussions with investment company leaders, and analysis of responses to its questionnaire mailing, the commission realized that studying only these companies would not be enough. In 1937 it expanded its study to include investment advisers, who were advising investment companies, investors, or both.

Members of an occupation category that had emerged after World War I and included many part-time practitioners—doctors and dentists as well as brokers and securities dealers—investment advisers had grown rapidly in number during the early 1930s. By 1937 there were more than 400—including quite a few who were regarded incompetent, if not dishonest.

In August 1940 the SEC's basic recommendations to register and regulate investment companies became law essentially as submitted to Congress. At committee hearings on the initial bill, industry representatives were virtually unanimous in urging its enactment, but some objected to portions of the measure. After the hearings, with the committees' encouragement, SEC and industry representatives agreed on proposed changes, which then were embodied in a substitute bill. Known as the Investment Company Act of 1940, it was unanimously passed by both houses of Congress and signed by President Roosevelt, to become effective November 1.

At the same time recommendations for the registration and regulation of investment advisers were incorporated in a companion bill, the Investment Advisers Act of 1940, which also was approved by Congress and the President.

To provide investors complete information on investment company activities, the Investment Company Act mandates complete disclosure of the companies' finances (including reports at least twice annually) and investment policies. To accord shareholders greater participation in management, the act prohibits mutual funds from changing the nature of their business or fundamental policies without the owners' approval.

The Act includes a number of provisions to ensure honest and unbiased fund management. Among other things, it prohibits persons guilty of securities frauds from serving as officers and directors; prevents underwriters, investment bankers, and brokers from constituting more than a minority of directors; requires SEC approval for any transactions between such companies and officers, directors, and other insiders, and asks companies to file all sales literature with the SEC.

To eliminate the possibility that investors could again lose money because of funds' drowning in debt, the Act severely limits the ability of investment companies to borrow.

The Investment Advisers Act requires advisers to disclose their background, nature of their business, financial condition, and bases for compensation, among other things, but does not give the SEC power to pass on applicants' qualifications. (It prohibits any individual or firm from calling himself/herself/itself "investment counsel" unless supervising investments is his/her/its principal business activity.) The Act authorizes the SEC to deny or revoke the registration of advisers convicted or enjoined because of misconduct arising from securities transactions.

By the end of the SEC's fiscal year on June 30, 1941, 436 investment companies—including 141 mutual funds—and 753 advisers had registered.

With investors better protected against abuses—if not against market risks—the legislation was expected to strengthen public trust and provide a new stimulus to mutual funds' growth as a stock market slide, under way since the beginning of 1939, continued.

In a way that no one could have predicted, circumstances changed. The U.S. entered World War II in December, and when the wartime bull market began four months later, the mechanism to regulate funds was in place. Throughout the war years the number of mutual funds being formed was approximately matched by the number going out of business, leaving the total essentially unchanged. (Owing to a net decrease in closed-end funds, this sufficed to enable mutual funds to pull ahead.) But thanks to rising stock prices, the industry's total assets doubled by the time the bull market ended several months after the armistice.

Stock prices advanced very little for the rest of the decade, but funds' total assets continued to grow as industry sales of new shares rose to an annual rate of $300 million or more, well ahead of redemptions. New mutual funds were being organized at a rate of about eight yearly—almost double the rate for closed-end funds. Although still primarily invested in common stocks, a few were of the "balanced" type. Investment policies showed increasing innovation. A few new funds adopted timing formulas for buying and selling stocks. One fund stated it would invest only in small companies, while another undertook to limit its investments to companies within its state of incorporation.

VIGOROUS GROWTH BEGINS

The mutual fund industry first experienced really vigorous growth in the 1950s. A period characterized by volatility in both the stock market and the economy at large—but also by fairly stable consumer prices, low interest rates, and solid expansion—the decade ended with stock prices up more than 250%. As the number of mutual funds increased over 50%, total industry assets rose eightfold, thanks about equally to net sales of shares and to considerable appreciation of the funds' investments.

With notable prescience, a few funds were organized in 1950 for the purpose of investing shareholders' money in what the SEC annual report referred to as "so-called growth stocks." Perhaps the best known of these was the T. Rowe Price Growth Stock Fund, first of the family of funds sponsored by the Baltimore investment counseling firm of T. Rowe Price. His growth stock theory of investing—based on the belief that one can best offset inflation by owning stocks of companies whose earnings are growing faster than inflation and faster than the economy—became widely adopted and adapted.

Brokers and dealers appeared as direct sponsors and investment advisers of funds, which they formed primarily as an investment medium for the firms' customers. They charged only nominal or no sales loads, in contrast with other funds, sponsored by investment counseling firms and others, which charged sales loads of up to 8.5% to provide brokers and dealers an incentive to sell the shares. The principle of charging no load at all was not new, however. It had been pioneered in 1928 by the investment counseling firm of Scudder, Stevens & Clark, which regarded it as an accommodation for clients wishing to invest in the predecessor of its Scudder Income Fund.

A variety of new investment objectives were pursued by funds organized during the decade. Among these were international investing (beginning with funds specializing in Canadian securities) and securities of companies engaged in natural resources development, electronics, atomic energy, automation, and life insurance. Other new objectives included investment primarily for income, in put and call options, and in "special situations."

Expansion of the fund industry and rising share prices spawned a significant increase in extravagant or misleading claims in advertisements and sales literature. This led the SEC and the National Association of Securities Dealers (NASD) to watch fund practices more closely and to study whether and how regulations might be tightened.

After discovering irregularities in accounts of one investment company, the SEC in 1956 began a regular program of inspections of a sampling of the industry. In ensuing years these inspections turned up a variety of violations of the 1940 Act, ranging from inadequate records and the failure to register, to prohibited affiliations of fund directors, improper selling practices, and the failure to advise shareholders of deviation from stated fundamental investment policies.

The industry's growth and the growing significance of mutual funds as holders of publicly traded stocks led the SEC, also in 1956, to launch a study of the effects of the companies' size. The commission wanted to see whether new legislation was required in light of whatever impact the funds' size might have on their own investment policies, on securities markets, and on companies in which they invested. The University of Pennsylvania's Wharton School of Finance and Commerce was asked to undertake the study, but it would be years before the results became known and recommendations for changes in regulations, if any, could be acted on.

THE "GO-GO" YEARS

The growth of mutual funds in the 1950s provided only a foretaste of the 1960s, a decade characterized by the longest—but not the steepest—bull market and the longest economic expansion in the country's recorded history.

Sharp drops in 1962 and 1966 notwithstanding, stock prices soared to unprecedented heights from late 1960 through 1968. On several occasions beginning in 1965, the Dow Jones Industrial Average approached 1000—and for a while on February 9, 1966 it actually managed to rise above that symbolic level—but the goal of a close above 1000 remained unattainable for this market cycle.

Despite disappointments along the way, Wall Street and Main Street worked themselves into a state of euphoria which reminded many of the 1920s. On the New York Stock Exchange alone, average daily volume rose from 3 to nearly 13 million shares and, in fact, on June 13, 1968 trading reached 21 million shares, breaking a record set on the day of the 1929 crash. (Visions of easy commission profits led to vigorous bidding for membership in the exchange, resulting in "seat" prices rising to a new high of $515,000—more than triple what they had sold for at the start of the decade.)

As turnover of listed shares rose to rates not seen in years, new shares were fed into the market in record volumes. Corporations eager to raise additional equity capital and owners of private companies eager to convert some of their shares into cash by going public took advantage of the demand for stocks. They registered new offerings with the SEC at an accelerating pace.

To handle the orders for this surge of business, brokerage firms almost doubled their legions of customers' men—only to find their back offices unable to keep up with the flow of paper. It wasn't only that record keeping lagged; millions of dollars worth of securities were misplaced or lost. By January 1968 daily trading hours had to be cut back, and eventually the trading week was shortened to four days. (The jam was not cleared until 1969, when trading volume fell as stock prices slumped.)

Millions who had never invested before were drawn into the market—often dealing with salesmen who were equally inexperienced and others who, in the SEC's words, would "seek to take advantage" of them. By the end of the decade, the New York Stock Exchange estimated, the number of stockholders in the United States had doubled.

The public was not only buying corporate equities. It was also investing heavily in mutual funds—so heavily that the sum of mutual funds' purchases and sales of stocks exceeded those of all other institutional investors, rising from less than $5 billion in 1959 to nearly $42 billion in 1969. Fund shares were being sold by thousands of fulltime and parttime sales representatives employed by large distribution organizations. The largest, Hamilton, had 7,800 sales representatives—mostly parttime—a number contrasted by an SEC study with the 2,200 registered representatives then employed by Merrill Lynch, the nation's largest broker-dealer.

How much the public's fund purchases were due to spontaneous, rational decisions and how much to sales pressure is not known. The pressures, to be sure, were strong as a number of fund organizers revived the practice of contractual plans, used in the 1920s, under which investors committed themselves to a schedule of share purchases that entailed payment of front-end loads as high as 50%.

With mutual funds leading the way, institutional investors had come to dominate activity on the Big Board. In both number and value of shares traded, the institutions' percentage, which had been much smaller than the public's in 1960, had pulled well ahead.

To accommodate—or stimulate—public demand, mutual funds were being created at the rate of a dozen or so a month, and competition for investors' dollars became intense among new and established funds.

Concern with short-run performance became paramount for many. It didn't seem to matter whether this goal was pursued by paying too much for the shares of a debt-ridden conglomerate or for a new issue—so long as a fund could sell them later to someone else who would pay even more.

The top performers became known as "go-go funds" inasmuch as the seemingly undisciplined approach of their portfolio managers, turning over large numbers of shares whenever they had short-run gains, was reminiscent of the abandon of performers engaged in "go-go" dancing. "Go-go" managers were hailed during the period of euphoria for their apparently unfailing ability to select only stocks that would go up, but they were eventually seen as being no more prescient than ordinary investors.

If anyone epitomized the era it was Gerald Tsai, who in 1957 had started the Fidelity organization's first growth fund, Fidelity Capital, and built it with impressive stock selection, fortuitous timing, and high turnover. In late 1965, while leading the fund to a year's gain of almost 50%—over five times the gain of the S&P 500—he quit Fidelity to start his own, the Manhattan Fund. Owing to the reputation he had developed at Fidelity, Manhattan's public offering in February 1966 was a smashing success: Some $247 million worth of shares were sold, several times what Tsai had expected.

Unfortunately for Tsai—and for the many who had bought Manhattan's shares—his timing was off. The market hit an air pocket, making 1966 the second worst year for stocks since World War II and causing Manhattan Fund shares to fall by year's end 14% below their public offering price. Although they came back during the market recovery of the next two years and advanced a bit, Tsai apparently had not regained his old touch and sold out his interest in his management company.

Worse off than Tsai's shareholders were those who had invested in funds that had bought "letter stock"—shares which had not been registered with the SEC and which, therefore, could not be resold. Until registered and thus marketable, letter stock was assigned values by fund management, not the market. Since they could be bought at a fraction of the cost of the same firms' registered shares, creative bookkeepers could assign values well above cost on funds' balance sheets. Thus they could inflate the share prices of the funds and give an exaggerated impression of their performance.

Perhaps the best known of the funds owning letter stock was the Mates Investment Fund. Founded by Frederic S. Mates in 1967 as the market roared back from the 1966 plunge, the fund's shares almost doubled in its first year and attracted so many new investors that Mates temporarily had to stop issuing them.

In late 1968 Mates bought the unregistered shares of a company called Omega Equities and carried them on his books at almost five times their cost, albeit below the market price of Omega's registered shares. To the public it appeared that Mates had made a large profit; indeed, his fund's performance led all others.

Unfortunately for Mates and his shareholders, the SEC subsequently stopped trading in Omega's registered shares. As Mates began to mark down the value of his unregistered shares, which accounted for some 20% of his fund's assets, shareholders besieged him with requests to redeem their shares. With too little cash to honor their requests, he asked and received the SEC's permission to suspend redemption temporarily, thereby depriving his shareholders of the right that is the heart of mutual fund share ownership.

As things turned out, the industry's record for investment performance in the 1960s was less impressive than its record for salesmanship. Of the more than $32 billion increase in its total net assets, almost two-thirds was attributable to net sales of shares, including those by the nearly 100 new funds organized during the period. By the end of the decade, share sales were running at an annual rate of almost $7 billion, up from $2 billion at the beginning, while redemptions stayed comfortably behind (Table 3-1).

So much money was coming into the funds that serious accounting and bookkeeping problems resulted. Some funds, overwhelmed and understaffed, could not determine the net asset values at which their shares should have been sold, causing investors to pay too much when buying shares and to receive too little when selling.

Throughout the 1960s, the SEC had tried—and failed—to end practices of some funds which, while boosting sales, had stained the industry's name. On the basis of the Wharton study, delivered in

TABLE 3-1. Mutual Funds' Capital Changes
(In Millions of Dollars)

Year	Share Sales	Redemptions	Net Capital Change
1941	$ 53	$ 45	$ 8
1942	73	25	48
1943	116	51	65
1944	169	71	98
1945	292	110	182
1946	370	144	226
1947	267	89	178
1948	274	127	147
1949	386	108	278
1950	519	281	238
1951	675	322	353
1952	783	196	587
1953	672	239	433
1954	863	400	463
1955	1,208	443	765
1956	1,347	433	914
1957	1,391	406	985
1958	1,620	511	1,109
1959	2,280	786	1,494
1960	2.097	842	1,255
1961	2,951	1,160	1,791
1962	2,699	1,123	1,576
1963	2,459	1,505	954
1964	3,403	1,874	1,529
1965	4,358	1,962	2,396
1966	4,672	2,005	2,667
1967	4,670	2,744	1,926
1968	6,820	3,839	2,981
1969	6,718	3,662	3,056
1970	4,626	2,988	1,638
1971	5,147	4,750	397
1972	4,893	6,563	(1,670)
1973	4,359	5,651	(1,292)
1974	3,092	3,381	(289)

TABLE 3-1. Continued

Year	Share Sales	Redemptions	Net Capital Change
1975	3,307	3,686	(379)
1976	3,885	6,777	(2,892)
1977	4,344	5,547	(1,203)
1978	4,893	6,173	(1,280)
1979	5,115	7.072	(1,957)
1980	8,237	7,215	1,022
1981	8,163	6,685	1,478
1982	12,252	6,875	5,377
1983	31,198	12,331	18,867
1984	36,024	15,876	20,148
1985	94,890	29,466	65,424
1986	175,969	57,956	118,013

Source: Investment Company Institute. Municipal bond funds excluded beginning with 1976.

1962, and a 1962–1963 study by its own staff, the SEC had recommended to Congress in 1967 a number of amendments to the 1940 Act.

Among the reforms which the commission deemed essential were: (1) imposition of a 5% maximum on mutual fund sales charges and (2) the elimination of the front-end load feature of contractual plans. The commission noted that, while fund underwriters had supported high sales loads to compete for dealers to sell their shares, the prevailing rates, running up to 8.5%, were clearly excessive.* Even 5%, the SEC said, exceeded sales charges generally prevailing in securities markets. As for the contractual plans, it detailed, among other things,

---

*The Investment Company Act did not limit sales charges for ordinary mutual funds to a percentage, but did impose a 9% ceiling on sales charges for periodic payment plan certificates. Many inferred from this that Congress intended mutual funds' loads to be capped at 9%, too.

the punitive nature of the steep front-end loads. They could result, the SEC said, in sales charges of up to 100% for investors who decided not to go through with their contracts.

Legislative relief was slow and partial. In 1968 and 1969, the Senate passed diluted versions of the SEC proposals in response to industry objections, but even this legislation got nowhere in the House of Representatives.

In 1970, a new bill was introduced in the House and, in amended form, was subsequently accepted by both houses and signed into law by President Nixon as the Investment Company Amendments Act of 1970.

Just as an earlier Congress and President had agreed not to specify a limit for loads—being content to sanction loads providing "reasonable compensation for sales personnel, broker-dealers, and underwriters" and "reasonable costs to investors"—so this Congress and President avoided definition of the term. Instead, they entrusted the industry with regulating itself via the National Association of Securities Dealers, whose members include both distributors affiliated with fund organizations and unaffiliated broker-dealers.

Contractual plan investors were given two choices. They could opt for a front-end load limit of 20% in any one year or a 50% load under which anyone wishing to cancel a contract early could get at least a partial refund.

About five more years had to pass before NASD directors and members agreed in 1975 on load recommendations in a form acceptable to the SEC, filed them with the SEC, obtained the SEC's approval, and declared them effective as of June 1, 1976. They included a new rule forbidding NASD members from selling shares of mutual funds if the sales charge exceeds 8.5% of the offering price.

YEARS OF DISAPPOINTMENT

Although, of course, no one could know it at the time, the bear market that was in its thirteenth month at the beginning of the 1970s provided an omen for the decade. Owners of stocks and bonds were in for years of disappointment as a result of events set in motion by recurring bursts of inflation.

First came the debt financing of our military expenditures for the Vietnam War, initiating a sequence of federal budget deficits that seems without end. (Fiscal 1969 had been the last year with a surplus, albeit a small one.) This was followed by the oil price escalation and production cutbacks of the Organization of Petroleum Exporting Countries and by OPEC's Arab members' embargo against the United States. Toward the end of the decade came the second oil "price shock."

The consequences of these events, and of the efforts by governments to cope with them, permeated the world. They were felt not only in production, employment, and international trade, but also in interest rates, currency exchange rates, and securities prices.

Inflation was so high, and total returns from financial assets were so low, that investors in stocks, bonds and even U.S. Treasury bills actually *lost* purchasing power during the period, according to a later analysis by Salomon Brothers. It was a time to be in nonfinancial assets such as oil, gold, U.S. coins, silver, stamps, and Chinese ceramics, which provided returns not only matching the 7.7% average increase in the cost of living but actually shooting as high as 34.7%.

Given the lack of precedent for the decade's events, and the unnerving swings in the U.S. economy and financial markets, it was difficult even for economically sophisticated people to know what to do. Many turned to some basic principles: When inflation runs wild, convert depreciating cash into "things," borrow as much as you can in the expectation you'll be repaying in inflated dollars, and go only into those financial assets which are most likely at least to maintain your purchasing power.

Those who had long held the belief that stocks were good hedges against inflation were surprised. The Dow Jones Industrial Average did crack the long elusive 1000 level in late 1972 and stay above it awhile, but by 1974 it had fallen below 600. For the decade as a whole, stock prices were up a mere 17%, excluding dividends, or

1.6% compounded per year. Adroit traders might have profited from the swings by buying and selling at the right times, but they would have had to be awfully good.

Mutual fund investors reacted to the markets' turbulence and to funds' disappointing performance in a predictable way. They sold. Stock and bond funds, whose assets had totaled $48.3 billion at the start of 1970, had to redeem shares totaling all of that and more; they had to pay out $52.6 billion in cash! What saved the funds, and succeeded in holding the drop in the funds' net assets for the whole decade to $2 billion, were $43.7 billion in sales of new shares—slightly above the previous decade's rate—and appreciation in the funds' investments of nearly $7 billion.

A major factor in new share sales was the formation of well over 100 new funds. The appeal of the higher interest paid on debt securities, which investors demanded to offset inflation, led to the creation of many income-oriented funds. They included a new category— the GNMA fund, which invested in mortgages backed by the Government National Mortgage Association. There also was a new flurry of interest in funds investing outside the United States, including the first of the funds concentrating in securities of Japan and other countries bordering the western Pacific Ocean.

The growing popularity of income-oriented funds, the disenchantment with stocks, and fund managers' defensive tactics led to a slight but perceptible shift in the division of total mutual fund assets. Stocks dropped from their customary 80 to 85% of total assets to below 75%, while the percentages of bond and cash equivalent holdings increased.

A large share of the money leaving equity funds found its way into a new form of financial instrument which was conceived in the inflationary environment of 1970 and subsequently has found wide acceptance: the mutual fund investing in money market securities, known as the money market fund.

Having seen interest rates rising with inflation in 1969, watching rates on Treasury bills cracking through 7% in 1970, and knowing that individual savings account depositors were limited to 5% or 5.25%, a few companies saw an opportunity for a new type of fund.

By enabling investors to buy interests in Treasury bills and other short-term instruments whose minimum denominations were too large for most individuals, a money market fund gave individuals easy access to securities whose yields protected them better against inflation and whose principal was safe. Free check writing added to their appeal. The first money market fund, Reserve Fund, offered its shares to the public in 1971, and the number of these funds quickly grew. By the end of the decade, there were 2.3 million accounts in 76 money market funds with assets totaling $45 billion, a large share of them offspring of mutual fund families and brokerage firms. Once they had put money in the money market funds' hands and had become accustomed to dealing with them, investors took advantage of the convenience of switching between money market funds and the firms' bond and stock funds.

By the end of the 1970s, inflation, due principally to the second oil price shock and rising unit labor costs, was out of control and financial markets were in disarray. The cost of living was rising at an accelerating rate, having climbed in less than one year from over 10% annually to over 15% annually, while the savings rate was falling. Banks had marked up their prime rates to over 15%, but Treasury bill yields remained at around 12%, providing returns that were *negative* in constant dollars but higher than those of long—and presumably riskier—bonds.

EMERGENCE OF A NEW INVESTMENT CLIMATE

With such memories of the 1970s still fresh, people faced the 1980s. What could they do to preserve the purchasing power of their savings and, if possible, earn a real return? If interest on savings accounts lagged inflation, stocks had failed to be a totally reliable inflation hedge every year, fixed-income securities lost value as interest rates rose, and investments in real estate and other hard assets involved liquidity and other problems, what were people to do?

The answers were not long in coming. In the absence of an effective fiscal policy, the Federal Reserve Board put the nation through two recessions in quick succession and squelched severe inflation (at least temporarily), thereby enhancing the attractiveness of financial assets again.

Mutual funds, as we will see, were to grow spectacularly in this new environment and mutual fund investors were to flourish. It may be useful, therefore, to recall in detail how it came about and whether it could have been foreseen.

By early 1980, as the longest peacetime business expansion in (recorded) U.S. history approached its fifth anniversary, consumer prices were rising at an annual rate of 18%, the highest since 1951, despite the restraint of monetary policy and a modest reduction in the federal deficit. Worse inflation news was widely expected.

As was learned later when statistics for early 1980 were calculated, the economic expansion had ended in January. A recession had already begun, owing to a tightening of credit markets, when the Fed and the Carter Administration took extraordinary measures to cool the economy.

By May, as the drop in industrial production gained momentum and unemployment reached 7.5%, the Federal Reserve and Administration began to loosen their reins. Interest rates already had been falling from their March peaks with the weakening of business conditions. In July, amid fears that a continuing decline in economic activity might presage a more severe recession than had yet materialized, the Fed cut the discount rate for the third consecutive month and lifted special credit controls.

Instead of becoming worse, however, the 1980 recession had ended—at six months, the shortest in U.S. history.

The economy did not merely bounce back from its sharpest quarterly drop of the postwar period and resume its growth. Stimulated by sharply lower interest rates, it expanded vigorously and inflationary pressures reemerged.

By September, when prices were rising at an annual rate of over 11%, the Federal Reserve had resumed, gradually but firmly, braking monetary growth. By the end of 1980, the Fed had increased its discount rate from 10 to 13% and restored a surcharge for large borrowers. Committed to squash inflation and determined not to risk premature relaxation (again), the Fed's Federal Open Market Committee (FOMC) established targets which provided for slower expansion of the nation's money supply in the following year.

Credit demands led to sharply higher interest rates in 1981—for those able and willing to borrow. In May the Fed raised its discount rate to a record 14%, and the surcharge to 4%, "to underscore the System's determination to curb excessive monetary expansion and thereby to exert a restraining influence on inflationary expectations." Yields of three-month Treasury bills soared to 16.75%. Thirty-year Treasury bonds—the safest long-maturity securities in the world— had to offer coupons of 14% so they could be sold. Banks raised the prime rate charged their most creditworthy customers to 20.5%; others had to pay even more.

The Federal Reserve Board, however, would not go higher. In mid-May, it rejected a request to raise the discount rate to 15% because it had noted indications that monetary growth was weakening.

The impact of high interest rates on employment and production became apparent when the economy turned down from its July peak, increasingly idling workers and plant capacity.

As the recession permeated the country, the Fed held firm. Between late September and December, it did roll back its rates slightly, but, aware of the perils of relaxing too much too soon and of being misunderstood, the Fed emphasized that it was not easing. These steps were only intended to keep its rates in line with short-term market rates. In fact, in July the FOMC had decided to reduce the rate of monetary growth further in 1982.

While prime, Treasury bill, and other short-term interest rates fell, long-term bond rates moved up if they moved at all. Investors, though aware that the rate of price increases had come down sharply with recession, doubted that the government would persevere to keep inflation down any more than it had done before. Thus they were reluctant to risk losing purchasing power by lending money for 20 or 30 years to anyone—including the U.S. Treasury—without an adequate inflation premium. At 13% long Treasury bonds offered them an extraordinary "real" return of around 9% above the inflation rate prevailing at the end of 1981.

Against this background the Federal Reserve Board sought to reassure the country. In its semiannual report to Congress in February 1982, it repeated its commitment to monetary restraint. To underscore the commitment, the FOMC reaffirmed its lower monetary growth targets for the year.

By the time the FOMC met on June 30, it had become increasingly concerned about the economic outlook and decided to take its first step toward ease. While adhering to its original target ranges for monetary growth rates for the year, the committee voted the next day to tolerate growth at the top of, or even above, its target ranges under certain circumstances. Since results of an FOMC meeting are not made public until after the next one, word of the action was not immediately disseminated. It was up to Fed watchers, as always, to scrutinize money market data in hopes of spotting what, if any, policy changes may have been adopted.

Market interest rates—especially short-term rates—fell during the first half of July as the Fed provided (nonborrowed) reserves to the banking system. There may have been those in the financial community who sensed a major turn in monetary policy and were acting on their analysis, but they did not say so very loudly. A sudden one-week bulge in the nation's money supply raised only limited and mild speculation.

On July 19 the Fed's moves became more visible. The Federal Reserve Board at last approved a reduction in the discount rate from 12% to 11.5%, the first cut since December and the first of seven to be made in 1982. The board merely said it took the action "in the context of recent declines in short-term market rates and the relatively restrained growth of money and credit in recent months."

The next day, in reviewing monetary policy before a Senate committee, Fed Chairman Paul A. Volcker disclosed and elaborated on the FOMC's action on monetary targets. "The evidence now seems to me strong that the inflationary tide has turned in a fundamental way," he said, citing not only small (3% per year) increases in consumer and producer prices but also a decline in the underlying trend of labor and other costs. And he added: ". . . more confidence (in the process of disinflation) should encourage greater willingness among investors to purchase longer debt securities."

While bond and stock prices rose slightly for the day, the common reaction to Volcker's testimony was that the Fed had not changed its tough policy. Moreover, concern was expressed that an upcoming Treasury refunding would cause interest rates to rise again.

Over the next several days, stock prices fell and interest rates drifted upward as the consumer price index for June showed a 1% increase and the Congressional Budget Office forecast widening federal deficits. Investors seemed to give up on the possibility of further Fed easing, especially when it was reported that Henry Kaufman of Salomon Brothers was forecasting that long-term bond interest rates would exceed 1981's 15.25% peak later in 1982 and short-term rates would come close to their record levels.

Then, when not expected, the Fed moved again, cutting the discount rate on July 30 to 11.5%. By this time word was spreading that the Fed had become more concerned about reviving the economy than about fighting inflation. Some noted that the money supply had been growing very slowly over the last three months, giving the Fed the opportunity to be more accommodating.

Such talk led some to suggest that the time may have come for increased investment in financial assets—in bonds, to lock in high yields and reap the benefit of capital gains as interest rates fell; in stocks, to take advantage of their relatively low price-earnings multiples and high yields.

But others found such suggestions premature. When unemployment of 9.8% was reported for July, a postwar record, concern about the economic outlook—including the prospects for corporate profits—became more intense. Fixed-income securities fluctuated in a narrow range, but stocks fell almost every day. "We're in a bear market," one analyst told *The New York Times*, "and it looks like we're going lower."

On August 12 rumors of another discount rate cut led fixed-income securities to rise significantly, but stocks fell slightly. The Dow Jones Industrial Average (DJIA) slipped 0.29 to 776.92, the eighth straight drop. Of the 18 trading sessions since the Fed cut its rate in mid-July, the stock average had fallen in 15 for a total of 49.18 points, or about 6%. One investment firm's managing director told reporters that the average could drop to 730, or another 6%. As things turned out, he could hardly have been more wrong; the DJIA has never again closed as low as 776.

On Friday, August 13, the DJIA recovered about 11 points, and debt securities rose again as more people got the impression that the Fed was vigorously pumping reserves into the banking system to stimulate the economy. The strong two-day rally in debt securities, which slashed Treasury bill yields from 9.9% to 8.9%, and 30-year government bond yields from about 13.3% to 12.8%, strengthened the conviction of those who anticipated even lower interest rates ahead. Newspapers reported a change in investor sentiment.

Thus, with little fanfare, was a bull market born. The fireworks were yet to come.

After the close of trading, the Federal Reserve did approve its third consecutive cut in the discount rate, giving analysts the weekend to study the implications.

On Monday, August 16, Albert M. Wojnilower of First Boston Corporation changed his interest rate forecast: Both short- and long-term rates would be lower next year. With the deterioration of the business outlook, he said, the risk of an increase in rates had diminished. Debt securities reacted with gains, and the DJIA rose 4.38 points.

Next day the rally was continuing when word reached Wall Street at lunchtime that Salomon Brothers' Kaufman had changed *his* forecast. He had taken a fresh look at the outlook for interest rates in light of eroding inflation expectations, poor prospects for economic recovery, and a contraction in business borrowing, and concluded that long-term bonds might fall from 12.5 to 9 to 10% within 12 months.

The stock market exploded. The Dow Jones average soared 38.81

points, its largest gain until then. Trading on the New York Stock Exchange exceeded 92 million shares, essentially equalling the record. Debt securities rose also, cutting about .5% off both short- and long-term rates.

With short-term debt securities leading the way in May, bonds following in July, and now stocks picking up in August, financial assets had embarked on a bull market of unusual intensity and endurance. Although many expressed doubts at the time—"I still feel the stock market is in a downtrend until you reach the give-up stage by investors," Merrill Lynch's Robert Farrell had told the *Times* on August 18—prices of bonds and stocks continued to rise.

Lured by soaring stock prices and by the opportunities to earn high total returns from bonds as interest rates continued falling, investors poured money into mutual funds. In the decade's first seven years, stock and bond funds' net assets increased nearly eightfold—to $353 billion (Table 3-2). Of the $307 billion increase since 1979, three-fourths was due to the net sales of new shares and one-fourth to appreciation of the funds' investments.

Not that fund investments were doing poorly. For five of the first seven years of the 1980s, at least one of the Lipper mutual fund indices, reflecting the larger members of broad fund groups, had total returns exceeding those estimated for the S&P 500 (Table 3-3). And, while for the period as a whole the broad market may have outperformed the Lipper fund indices, so did individual funds.

The number of stock and bond funds nearly tripled to more than 1,100 by the end of 1986 as fund sponsors created a seemingly endless variety of fund types—epitomized by sector funds—and as multifund families intensified their competition for investors' dollars across the board. Ironically, the SEC had relaxed restrictions on promotion and advertising just before the bull market got under way, providing funds with ample opportunity to entice prospects in periodicals and on radio and television.

It's worth noting that, even though stocks were in the news almost daily in the mid-1980s, as the market soared to new highs, mutual fund investors seemed more interested in bond funds—especially government bond funds—than ever before. Funds investing in gov-

TABLE 3-2. Growth of Mutual Funds

Year-end	Number of Funds	Net Assets in Billions	Year-end	Number of Funds	Net Assets in Billions
1924		*	1956	135	9.1
1925		*	1957	143	8.7
1926		*	1958	151	13.2
1927		*	1959	155	15.8
1928		$ .1	1960	161	17.0
1929		.1	1961	170	22.8
1930		.1	1962	169	21.3
1931		.1	1963	165	25.2
1932		.1	1964	160	29.1
1933		.2	1965	170	35.2
1934		.2	1966	182	34.8
1935		.4	1967	204	44.7
1936		.5	1968	240	52.7
1937		.4	1969	269	48.3
1938		.5	1970	356	47.6
1939		.5	1971	392	55.1
1940		.4	1972	410	59.8
1941	68	.4	1973	421	46.5
1942	68	.5	1974	416	34.1
1943	68	.7	1975	390	42.2
1944	68	.9	1976	404	47.6
1945	73	1.3	1977	395	42.8
1946	74	1.3	1978	409	42.4
1947	80	1.4	1979	402	46.3
1948	87	1.5	1980	416	55.5
1949	91	2.0	1981	440	52.2
1950	98	2.5	1982	489	70.0
1951	103	3.1	1983	575	100.2
1952	110	3.9	1984	710	118.6
1953	110	4.1	1985	896	213.4
1954	115	6.1	1986	1,109	353.3
1955	125	7.8			

* Less than .1 billion

Source: Investment Company Institute

Note: Data, which exclude money market and municipal bond funds, include only stock, bond, and income funds that belong to ICI.

98

TABLE 3-3. Total Returns for Mutual Funds and S&P 500 Stocks Compared 1980–86

Year-end	Growth Funds		Growth & Income Funds		Balanced Funds		Standard & Poor's 500 Composite	
	Index	Return	Index	Return	Index	Return	Index	Return
1980	163.47	+37.27%	226.31	+28.52%	187.71	+20.68%	135.76	+32.56%
1981	149.73	− 8.42	221.38	− 2.18	182.43	− 2.81	122.55	− 4.89
1982	180.04	+20.24	267.15	+20.68	231.11	+26.68	140.64	+21.57
1983	220.13	+22.27	329.78	+23.44	270.25	+16.94	164.93	+22.59
1984	213.98	− 2.79	338.44	+ 2.63	283.44	+ 4.88	167.24	+ 6.29
1985	278.89	+30.34	432.18	+27.70	361.25	+27.45	211.28	+31.79
1986	323.11	+15.86	502.04	+16.17	429.95	+19.02	242.17	+18.71
Cumulative Beginning of 1980 through end of 1986		171.32%		185.10%		176.42%		212.04%

Source: Annual data, Lipper Analytical Services, Inc., *Lipper—Mutual Fund Performance Analysis;* cumulative returns, Lipper Analytical Services, Inc.

Note: Lipper's mutual fund indices are adjusted for the reinvestment of capital gains distributions and dividends. Returns shown for the S&P 500 reflect Lipper's calculation of reinvested dividends for the group as well as the index change. Lipper's method differs slightly from that used by Standard & Poor's Corporation itself.

TABLE 3-4. Where Mutual Fund Investors Put Their Money

Investment Objectives of Funds	Net Assets in Billions									
	1977	1978	1979	1980	1981	1982	1983	1984	1985	1986
Aggressive Growth	$ 2.2	$ 2.3	$ 3.0	$ 4.7	$ 5.0	$ 9.6	$18.7	$ 14.2	$ 20.1	$ 25.0
Growth	11.7	11.4	13.0	16.8	15.2	19.0	26.0	26.7	35.1	43.7
Growth & Income	16.1	15.2	16.5	19.5	18.2	22.0	29.3	31.6	45.0	65.9
Precious Metals	NA	NA	NA	NA	NA	NA	NA	.4	1.5	2.0
International	NA	NA	NA	NA	NA	NA	NA	5.2	8.0	15.9
Balanced	4.1	3.7	3.4	3.4	2.8	3.1	3.1	2.9	4.1	7.5
Income	4.4	4.6	4.5	4.8	4.5	5.9	8.8	7.1	11.0	18.3
Option Income	.3	.4	.5	.6	.6	.8	1.9	3.4	5.6	7.0
Government Income }	4.0	4.7	5.1	5.7	5.9	9.1	11.3	6.4	40.0	81.9
Corporate Bond								14.6	24.0	41.5
GNMA	--	--	--	--	NA	NA	NA	4.0	17.9	39.8
Total	42.8	42.4	46.0	55.5	52.1	69.4	99.0	116.3	212.3	348.5

Source: Investment Company Institute
Notes: Totals may not add due to rounding.

ernment securities, for which the Investment Company Institute had not even bothered to publish data when the decade began, had grown to $82 billion in assets and moved ahead of the $66 billion in the long popular growth and income funds (Table 3-4). This group continued to expand and attract investors' money, but its share of total equity and bond fund assets has been declining throughout the 1980s (Figure 3-1). Growth and aggressive growth funds, according to ICI, also have

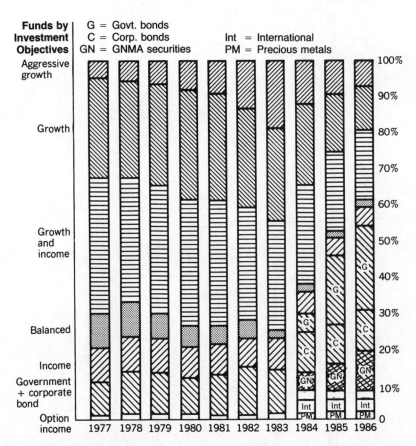

Figure 3-1. Where Mutual Fund Investors Put Their Money (percentages of total fund assets). Data source: Investment Company Institute.

TABLE 3-5. How Stock and Bond Funds Invest Their Money (Assets in Billions)

Investment	At Year-end									
	1977	1978	1979	1980	1981	1982	1983	1984	1985	1986
Cash & equivalent	$ 3.3	$ 4.5	$ 5.0	$ 5.3	$ 5.3	$ 6.0	$ 8.3	$12.0	$20.6	$30.7
Corporate bonds	6.5	5.6	5.6	6.6	7.5	10.8	13.1	15.0	25.0	47.3
Preferred stocks	.4	.4	.4	.5	.4	1.6	1.5	1.6	3.8	7.4
Common stocks	30.8	30.7	34.3	41.6	36.7	47.7	72.9	81.6	119.7	153.7
Government bonds	1.3	1.1	.8	1.4	2.2	3.8	3.9	8.0	43.5	111.5
Other	.6	.2	.2	.1	.2	.1	.5	.4	.9	2.7
Total	42.8	42.4	46.3	55.5	52.2	70.0	100.2	118.6	213.4	353.3

Source: Investment Company Institute

Note: Totals may not add due to rounding.

been growing considerably but have not been able to maintain the shares of total fund assets which they had attained early in the decade's bull market.

Looking at the division of funds' assets by the types of securities in which they invested, instead of by classification of investment objectives, one can more easily see the change that has taken place (Table 3-5 and Figure 3-2). Investments in both common stocks and long-term government bonds rose by more than $110 billion from year-end 1980 to year-end 1986. But for common stocks this resulted in a

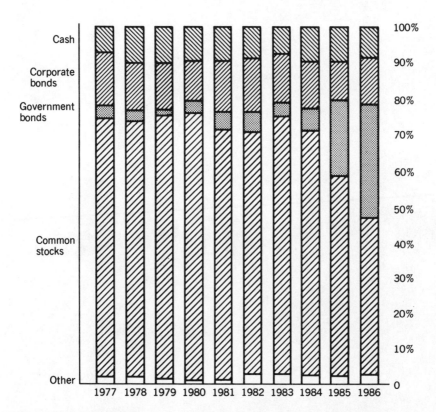

Figure 3-2. How Stock and Bond Funds Invest Their Money (percentages of total fund assets). Data source: Investment Company Institute.

fall of over 30 percentage points—from 75% of total assets to 43.5% while long-term government bonds gained roughly the share which stocks lost, rising from 2.5% to 31.6%. Shares of fund assets accounted for by cash and equivalents, corporate bonds, preferred stock, and other securities held essentially constant.

4

CHOOSING YOUR
FIRST FUND

Regardless of whether you plan to invest a
lot or a little in mutual funds, you have to
start with one. After finding and investing
in the one that seems to be the most suitable, you can and should add one or more
to your portfolio, depending on your financial assets.

But don't rush. You're in this for the long
term, remember, and will want to become
adjusted to the experience of patient, disciplined investing in a continuously changing market environment.

In this chapter, we will first concentrate
on identifying the initial fund, then suggest
how to invest in it. In the next chapter, we
will discuss the question of how many funds

to be in and outline how to spot the other(s) that would meet your requirements.

Your first fund is one that you should be able to live with in comfort. That's why we will be saying a lot in this chapter about controlling risk. We'll talk later about finding opportunities to increase your gains—after you feel you can put assets at risk because you're acting on judgment, not hunches or compulsion.

The approach begins with a few simple steps—tests which you can apply to a small group of promising funds that stand out from the approximately 900 equity funds. We don't know, of course, which fund will emerge as your leading prospect when you apply these tests, but we're pretty confident it'll fit a certain pattern: low volatility, reliable track record over a long period, and a steady portfolio manager. A fund with such attributes should get you started toward your financial goals.

APPLYING THE SCREENS

Step 1: Historic Performance

Since we are concerned with how well your portfolio will serve you for years to come, we confine our consideration to funds that have the best long-term performance records. Of all the meaningful indicators of future success, historic long-term performance data probably have the greatest predictive value. A glance at Table 4-1 will make clear the risks of randomly picking a fund from among the best performers of only the most recent year. But, as we will see, even historic data are only partially reliable as a guide to future performance.

Before proceeding, let us agree on the definition of a word that you'll meet over and over again when you read about mutual funds: performance. While this word has several meanings in ordinary conversation, it has been given one precise definition in the world of mutual funds: total return. This, in turn, is defined as the sum of (1) the increase or decrease of a fund's net asset value (NAV) per share during a given period and (2) the total of capital gains and dividend

TABLE 4-1. What Can Happen to One Year's Leaders

Fund	Rank 1985	1986	Fund	Rank 1985	1986
Fidelity Overseas	1	7	Oppenheimer Challenger	13	876
Fidelity Over the Counter	2	636	Twentieth Century Gift	14	76
New England Zenith Capital Growth	3	1	Transatlantic	15	19
Paine Webber Atlas	4	44	Oppenheimer AIM	16	27
Putnam International	5	48	Quasar	17	660
Alliance International	6	33	Scudder International	18	21
FT International	7	14	Shearson Global	19	63
Neuberger & Berman Hemisphere	8	*	GIT Special Growth	20	401
Fidelity Select Health	9	136	IDS Strategy Aggressive Equity	21	114
GAM International	10	26	Loomis-Sayles Capital	22	75
Fidelity Select Leisure	11	364	IDS International	23	17
Kemper International	12	32	ABT Emerging Growth	24	520
			Vanguard Special Health	25	147

*Merged into Neuberger & Berman Manhattan Fund
Source: Lipper Analytical Services, Inc., *Lipper—Mutual Fund Performance Analysis.*

distributions per share for the same period. Although some people may take either or both distributions in cash because they need the money, for purposes of inter-fund comparison it is assumed that both distributions were subsequently reinvested in shares, which then also rose or fell.

(Experts differ in how they calculate reinvestment. Some assume it occurred on the day of the distributions; others assume it took place later, such as the end of the particular month. We prefer the former because it's more realistic. In the long run, it doesn't matter very much.)

To get usable data for our assessment of funds' past performance, we fortunately can utilize independent sources—statistical services, periodicals, and newsletters—which scrutinize the industry. They do the difficult job of adjusting individual funds' figures when necessary to make them comparable with others. It would be impossible for any of us alone to obtain data from each fund and compile them for identical periods in a way that ensures we'll be comparing apples and apples, not apples and oranges.

Since the phrase "long-term" is a bit vague, let us define it as well: five years or more.

Because we prefer to have two check points, and because fund reporting services make performance data readily available for periods of 5 and 10 years, we have chosen these for demonstrations of fund excellence. If 5 years is not a long enough period to include one complete stock market cycle, 10 years should suffice. To have been successful over 5 or 10 years, a fund will have had to do more than lead a market rally; even more important, it will have had to avoid any losses of significance.

The source which we find most convenient, complete, and economical for 5- and 10-year mutual fund performance data is *Barron's*, the weekly published by Dow Jones & Company, Inc.

Every three months—about six weeks after the end of each calendar quarter—*Barron's* publishes a wealth of mutual fund statistics which are provided by Lipper Analytical Services, Inc. They include not

only a variety of performance and other data for more than 1,200 mutual funds, but also tables listing the 25 funds that led in total return
for several periods—including 5 and 10 years—ending with the latest
quarter (Figure 4-1).

Using these lists and a crude point system, you begin with the first
screen (Table 4-2). Give 25 points to every one of the top 25 funds
for the latest 10 years except for those which have an "x" next to their
names. Each of those is closed to new investors. Some may welcome
you one day, but for now you need not spend time on them.

Next, while continuing to ignore the closed funds, you assign 25
points to each of the top performers for the latest 5 years.

Any funds to which you've given 50 points should catch your eye.

Step 2: Down Year Performance

You next submit the funds with 50 points to the first hurdle: down
year performance exceeding that of the S&P 500.

You'll be able to find no-load funds' performance data for the most
recent down year—as this was written, it was 1981, when the S&P
500's total return was a negative 5.0%—in annuals such as the American Association of Individual Investors' *Guide to No-Load Mutual
Funds, Dow Jones-Irwin No-Load Mutual Funds,* and *The Handbook
for No-Load Fund Investors,* which also includes certain low-load
funds. If you wish to consider the broader universe of funds, check
CDA Mutual Fund Report, Mutual Fund Sourcebook, or Wiesenberger Financial Services' annual. Of course, with a bit more effort,
you also can get data from the funds themselves, but they may not
be comparable with one another. (They may not all be based on calendar years, for example.)

As Table 4-3 illustrates for the years ended in 1986, you'll soon
discover that some funds which did well in the 5-year period, but
were not listed for 10 years, are too new to have made any kind of a
record in the latest down year. Skip them.

You want only to consider those funds which were in business dur-

TOP FUNDS OVER TIME

TEN YEARS 6/30/77 to 6/30/87		FIVE YEARS 6/30/82 to 6/30/87		ONE YEAR 6/30/86 to 6/30/87		SIX MONTHS 12/31/86 to 6/30/87		2nd QUARTER 3/31/87 to 6/30/87	
Fidelity Magellan Fund	1,794.97%	Merrill Lyn Pacific	485.97%	USAA Gold	127.17%	Sherman, Dean Fund	68.70%	Dreyfus Strat Agg Inv LP	42.51%
20th Century Growth	1,130.39	Vanguard World-Intl Gro	384.52	Van Eck Gold/Resources	126.23	DFA UnitedKingdomSmCo	67.99	Sherman, Dean Fund	31.94
International Investors	1,109.31	BBK International	374.98	IDS Precious Metals	121.54	New Eng Zenith Cap Gro	67.25	DFA UnitedKingdomSmCo	22.29
Twentieth Century Select	1,094.47	Fidelity Magellan Fund	367.34	US New Prospector	116.79	Van Eck Gold/Resources	65.27	DFA Japan Small Company	21.66
Amer Capital Pace	1,021.89	Putnam Intl Equities	355.93	Franklin Gold Fund	113.64	Franklin Gold Fund	58.65	GT Japan Growth	20.23
Loomis-Sayles Capital x	1,008.87	Loomis-Sayles Capital x	336.19	Hutton Inv Sr-Prec Met	109.69	IDS Precious Metals	57.39	Nomura Pacific Basin	18.98
Franklin Gold Fund	961.63	T Rowe Price Intl Fund	320.20	Vanguard Special-Gold	108.75	US New Prospector	56.49	Equity Strategies x	18.87
Quasar Associated x	942.75	Alliance Technology	315.41	Keystone Prec Metals	108.05	Colonial Adv Str Gold	55.36	Fidelity Sel Enrgy Ser	18.32
Weingarten Equity	931.04	Fidelity Sel Health	307.02	US Prospector Fund x	107.55	US Prospector Fund x	54.93	Newport Far East	18.14
Lehman Capital Fund	919.44	Scudder International	306.11	US Gold Shares	105.96	Criterion Technology	50.59	Templeton Foreign	13.70
Merrill Lyn Pacific	915.29	Fidelity Destiny I	295.86	Financial Port-Gold	103.21	MFS Lifetime Mgd Sectr	50.16	Newport Global Growth	13.58
Amev Growth Fd	898.25	Weingarten Equity	291.34	Colonial Adv Str Gold	101.15	Fidelity Sel Enrgy Ser	50.12	Trustees Commingled Intl	12.57
New Eng Growth Fund	879.05	Vanguard Qual Dvd I x	286.88	Fidelity Sel Prec-Mtls	96.44	Keystone Prec Metals	50.01	First Inv International	12.14
Phoenix Stock	843.37	Alliance International	285.88	Oppenheimer Gld & Sp Min	92.23	USAA Gold	49.40	Financial Port-Pacific	11.48
Evergreen Fund	836.64	Manhattan Fund	280.28	Strategic Investments	89.24	Fidelity Sel Prec-Mtls	47.98	Criterion Global Growth	11.22
Lindner Fund x	835.86	Windsor Fund x	279.55	Golconda Investors Ltd	88.59	Vanguard Special-Gold	47.62	Financial Port-Energy	11.12
US Gold Shares	816.35	Legg Mason Value Trust	278.03	International Investors	88.12	Hutton Inv Sr-Prec Met	47.12	Europacific Growth	10.82
IDS Growth Fund	781.68	Phoenix Growth	276.97	Sherman, Dean Fund	87.29	Financial Port-Gold	47.00	Freedom Global	10.78
Constellation Growth	753.19	Fairmont Fund	272.86	Lexington Goldfund	86.81	Alliance Technology	46.29	United Intl Growth	10.60
Nicholas Fund	752.86	Lehman Opportunity	272.74	United Gold & Government	82.84	Shearson Lehman Pr Met	46.06	Shearson Lehman Pr Met	10.32
Growth Fund of America	738.88	United Intl Growth	272.69	Midas Gold Shs & Bullion	79.62	Golconda Investors Ltd	45.96	T Rowe Price Intl Fund	10.20
Tudor Fund	733.68	Phoenix Stock	270.45	New Eng Zenith Cap Gro	77.87	Lexington Goldfund	45.62	Fidelity Europe	10.14
Amer Special Fd	729.78	Guardian Park Avenue	270.24	DFA UnitedKingdomSmCo	74.85	MFS Lifetime Emer Gro	45.54	North Star Apollo	10.01
Fidelity Destiny I	726.19	Princor Capital Accum	269.59	Merrill Lyn Natrl Res	70.34	Midas Gold Shs & Bullion	45.25	Fundtrust Intl	9.87
United Vanguard Fund	721.04	United Income	268.30	Financial Port-Pacific	69.84	United Gold & Government	45.05	Ivy International	9.71

Figure 4-1. The Top 25 Funds for Various Periods. Source: Lipper Analytical Services, Inc., as it appeared in *Barron's* August 10, 1987.

110

TABLE 4-2. Fund Performance Screen

Criteria	Weight
Top 25 ranking in latest 5-year period	25 points
Top 25 ranking in latest 10-year period	25 points
Performance exceeding S&P 500 in most recent down year	50 points

ing the latest down year and proved their potential for you by doing better than the S&P 500—by going down less or by not going down at all.

Doing well when stock prices are rising is not a particularly impressive achievement, but even then not every fund manager or investor can claim it. (In the first four-plus years of the phenomenal bull market that began in 1982, at least eight funds had a *negative* total return!) What *is* impressive—and, indeed, crucial, to long-term success in investing—is avoiding or minimizing portfolio damage when stock prices are falling. You want a fund manager who has demonstrated the ability to do *that*—and *still* has the knack.

Worse-than-average performance in a down year, usually due to the risky nature of a fund's portfolio, should persuade you to stay clear of the fund. The odds against its recovering from a market slump are high because it is obliged to take even greater risks in hope of exceptional increases in its portfolio.

A fund manager who has suffered a 25% drop has to manage a 33⅓% increase to get even; one who has suffered a 33⅓% loss has to gain 50%. We don't need to spell out the risks a manager would have to take, with your money, to try to achieve increases of such magnitudes. And that would be only to get even—not exactly what you're paying the manager for.

Consider what such a fund manager probably has had to face. To score impressive gains when the market was up, he had to be essentially 100% invested in stocks. When the market dropped, taking his holdings down along with the rest, his shareholders panicked. They

TABLE 4-3. Leading Performers for 10, 5, and Latest Down Years

	10 Years Ended 1986	5 Years Ended 1986	1981
American Capital Pace	x	o	ok
AMEV Growth	x	o	no
BBK International[a]	o	x	ok
Eaton Vance Total Return	o	x	new
Evergreen Fund	x	o	ok
Evergreen Total Return	o	x	ok
Fairmont.Fund	o	x	ok
Fidelity Destiny I	x	x	ok
Fidelity Magellan	x	x	ok
Fidelity Select Financial	o	x	new
Fidelity Select Health	o	x	new
Franklin Gold	x	o	no
Growth Fund of America	x	o	ok
IDS Growth	x	o	ok
International Investors	x	o	no
Lehman Capital	x	o	ok
Lindner Dividend [c]	x	x	ok
Lindner Fund [c]	x	o	ok
Loomis-Sayles Capital [c]	x	x	ok
Merrill Lynch Pacific	x	x	ok
NEL Growth	x	x	ok
New York Venture	x	o	ok
Nicholas Fund	x	o	ok
Over-the-Counter Securities	x	o	ok
Phoenix Growth	o	x	ok
Phoenix Stock	x	x	ok
Price (T. Rowe) International	o	x	ok
Prudential Bache Utility	o	x	new
Putnam International Equities	o	x	ok
Quasar Associates [c]	x	o	no
Quest for Value	o	x	ok
Strong Investment	o	x	new
Strong Total Return	o	x	new
Twentieth Century Growth	x	o	no

	10 Years Ended 1986	5 Years Ended 1986	1981
Twentieth Century Select	x	o	ok
United Continental Income	o	x	ok
United Income	o	x	ok
United Services Gold Shares	x	o	no
Value Line Leveraged Growth	x	o	ok
Vanguard Qualified Dividend I ᶜ	o	x	ok
Vanguard World—International Growth	o	x	new
Washington Mutual	o	x	ok
Weingarten Equity	x	o	no

x = among top 25 performers, o = not among top 25, ok = 1981 total return exceeded S&P 500, no = 1981 total return lagged S&P 500, new = fund not in operation for all of 1981.
a = not available to public
c = closed to new investors
Sources: 10- and 5-year performance, Lipper Analytical Services, Inc., as it appeared in *Barron's* February 16, 1987; 1981 performance, various publications.

wanted cash. To raise the cash necessary to redeem shares, he had to sell off bits of his portfolio at the worst time—when prices were down.

Funds which beat the S&P 500 in a down year are likely to have significant percentages of their assets in cash and in well-diversified portfolios of stocks which pay high dividends. They hold the cash in anticipation of redemption requirements as well as for purchases of stocks at depressed prices when they, perhaps ahead of others, perceive the dawn of recovery.

Add another 50 points for the funds that made the grade, and you're ready to submit to the next screen the funds which got at least 75 points. Showing up in both 5- and 10-year periods is not essential to qualifying a fund for your consideration, but above-average down year performance is.

TABLE 4-4. Fund and Manager Profile Screen

Criteria	Weight
Same manager who made the record	50 points
Asset allocation of 20% or more in cash	25 points
Fund net assets less than $1 billion	25 points

Step 3: The Portfolio Manager

Having identified a few funds for your possible investment, you'll now want to compare three of their major attributes to narrow the search, beginning with the portfolio manager (Table 4-4).

Relatively few funds do what we—and, we assume, you—want your portfolio to do: outperform the S&P 500 for periods of 5 years or more. (Only one in four did so for the 5 years ended in 1986.) Those that do are usually run by managers who try to avoid the kind of risk-taking which could place them in a leaders' slot for a quarter year—but probably not longer. Funds that lead in performance during market rallies—often merely regaining part of what was lost in the last market decline—are rarely listed among the top performers over periods as long as 3 or 5 years.

A fund's investment policy may be adopted by its board of directors (or trustees), and the firm contracted to be the investment adviser may have the responsibility of implementing the policy. But it is the manager who converts policy into the day-to-day decisions—to buy, sell, or hold—which are responsible for success or failure.*

Within the guidelines of board policy and the investment advisory contract, the portfolio manager must exercise judgment in a number

---

*These distinctions are not applicable, of course, in cases in which one person is portfolio manager, controlling stockholder of the adviser, and chief executive officer of the fund.

of ways. Of greatest interest to us when selecting a fund are the following:

What percent of assets should be invested in common stocks, bonds (if any), and cash equivalents (i.e., temporary investments such as U.S. Treasury bills, commercial paper, or certificates of deposit).

Which sectors of the economy should be more heavily represented among the stocks and which less.

Which companies in an industry should be included in the fund's portfolio—on what basis—and which should be avoided.

When should securities be bought and when should they be sold.

It is most important, therefore, to determine whether the portfolio manager who is responsible for the fund's good record is still in charge. Since neither the Investment Company Act nor the SEC require a fund to provide its portfolio manager's identity or length of tenure in its prospectus or periodic reports—and since most don't volunteer this information—you'll probably have to ask for it by telephone when you request these publications (see box).

INFORMATION FROM FUNDS

You can get performance data for all funds, calculated on a uniform basis, from independent reporting services, and you should easily be able to obtain all other important information on each fund by reading its printed materials and by making telephone inquiries.

Of the various printed documents with which you should become familiar, the most important is the prospectus, as discussed in Chapter 2. Among other things, it states the fund's investment objectives and policy, describes its management, provides historic per-share financial information, describes the relationship with the investment adviser, and explains how to buy and redeem the fund's shares. Some funds also include balance sheets and lists of investments in their prospectuses; others publish these in the periodic reports. Because mutual fund shares

---

are offered continuously, the prospectus is updated when changes in major data make it necessary.

Whether wishing to save on printing costs or feeling that shareholders wouldn't be interested, some funds limit the information in the prospectus to the little that the SEC requires and publish more in the statement of additional information that is made available on request. If that's the case with a fund you're considering, it will be necessary for you to ask for one of these statements as well.

For more current balance sheets, portfolios, lists of securities bought and sold, and comments on the fund's performance, you'll want the most recent annual, semiannual, and/or quarterly reports.

The volumes and quality of prose and data vary greatly among funds. After scanning a few fund documents, you'll quickly realize how similarly performing funds differ in investment strategies and portfolio composition. (Mutual Shares, for example, lists more types of securities than most others. In addition to the usual stocks and bonds, its report also shows bonds of companies in reorganization and stocks of companies involved in mergers or liquidation.)

To get information not available in print, or to be sure that what you have is up-to-date, you should follow up by telephoning each fund you're considering.

You should especially call to ensure that the portfolio manager is still directing the fund's investment strategy, and that the investment adviser and policy remain unchanged. Even if the name has recently appeared in a fund annual, fund newsletter, magazine, or newspaper, you'll want to confirm that there has been no change since publication.

While you have fund personnel on the phone, inquire about loads and other charges. It's possible that you missed a fee by reading the prospectus too hastily or that one has been imposed since you received it.

Be aware that you may have to be firm to get across the point that you want, and are entitled to have, publicly disseminated information about the funds you are considering. Most of the people you get when you dial funds' 800 numbers try to be helpful, but not all seem to understand or to have at hand what you're after.

Be prepared, by the way, for delays in getting through to the fund (especially at lunchtime and during the peak of IRA season). You'll get a busy signal more than you'd like—especially when trading is active—or you'll get the recorded "all our representatives are busy," then wind up listening—if you're lucky—to chamber music. But sooner or later you will get through. Reaching the fund promptly may be important to you after you have invested when you want to buy or sell, or when you want to know whether a fund has received your check, your redemption request, or some other directive. Thus, you may wish to ask if the fund has a number that you can dial directly—at your expense. If the fund is a good performer, you won't mind the cost of an occasional long distance call.

If you find out that the person who built the record which drew it to your attention is still managing the fund's portfolio, you can assume that he or she has dealt satisfactorily with these and other questions. You have no guarantee, of course, that the manager will continue to do as well. Unless the fund has become too big (see following text), or the market environment changes to one in which the manager has no experience, you should have confidence that your money is in good hands.

If you learn that a new manager is running the portfolio, you probably will want to forget the fund. With a new person in charge, you simply have no basis for judging how that fund is likely to fare under various circumstances. In the long run bypassing such fund may turn out to have been unfair to the new manager and to yourself, but fairness is not the point; you're trying to limit your exposure to risk as you undertake to invest your money.

Step 4: Asset Allocation

In describing a fund's investment policy and objectives, a prospectus states whether the fund is seeking income, capital appreciation, or both (and, if the latter, whether one more than the other). It also cites the types of securities the fund may buy and whether there are minimums or maximums for any category.

Within these guidelines, the portfolio manager has to decide how to allocate and reallocate the fund's assets among cash and the various types of securities in response to changing market conditions.

Asset allocation, to a large extent, determines how high a fund's shares can rise in a bull market, and how well insulated the fund is against a market collapse. That's because it is the principal tool for dealing with the first of the three major types of risk inherent in stock ownership: the risk associated with the stock market as a whole. (For the other two risks, see box on next page).

Studies have indicated that, depending on the industry, from 25% to 60% of the changes in stock prices over time can be attributed to general market movements. To moderate this market risk, portfolio managers may invest in other assets which do not move in step with stocks—principally cash equivalents, but also fixed-income securities, including convertibles, as seems appropriate.

Knowing how a fund's assets are allocated tells you the types and extent of risks the portfolio manager is able or willing to assume to achieve the fund's stated objective.

If you have found a fund which made it to the top of the heap with as much as 20% of its assets in cash, you probably have spotted a portfolio manager who has a gift for stock selection and little inclination or need to take high risk. Such a fund could be a real winner for you.

If, on the other hand, a fund has performed very well while having a high percentage of assets invested in common stocks, you may assume the manager has been taking a high risk—and has been successful. You will have a found a fund which is likely to do beautifully during an up market. It, however, also could fare as poorly as the S&P 500—or worse—during a down market if the asset allocation is not changed. (Some funds have policies of deliberately remaining 99% or so invested in stocks, regardless of what the market is doing.)

By looking at the data on asset allocation in a fund's prospectus or periodic report, or in a service such as the *CDA Mutual Fund Report*, you'll get a pretty good idea of how well the fund can deal with market

WHERE STOCK SELECTION COMES IN

In addition to market risk, every investor in stocks also incurs two other risks: one associated with any particular industry or other group of companies having a common denominator, and one associated with any individual company. These risks are dealt with in stock selection.

We do not include them in our screens because we feel that our criteria suffice as a disciplined means of finding one fund in a handful of funds whose performance had lifted them from among some 900. Naturally, a portfolio manager's stock selection and industry weighting skills are very important. Therefore, we suggest that you try to assess them to help you select one fund when two or more emerge from your screens as candidates. To judge how well each is prepared to cope with industry and company risks in the future, consider the mix of industries and companies in its portfolio.

A fund's list of stocks will show how well diversified it is—how vulnerable it might be to a drop in the fortunes of a particular industry or company. The latest periodic report, listing recent purchases and sales, may indicate if a change in emphasis is under way.

Determine how many industries each fund is in, which industry constitutes its largest holding, and what the percent of the holding is. See whether you agree with the portfolio's relative proportions of industries benefiting from inflation and those punished by it, of capital-intensive companies whose profitability is significantly affected by interest rates and companies that borrow little or nothing. And so on.

Then see whether you feel each fund is sufficiently diversified by owning shares in several companies within each listed industry, in order to minimize exposure to the unhappy surprises that can befall any individual firm.

Ironically, a fund also can be too well diversified to give you superior performance. If it is as broadly diversified as "the market"—and not an index fund (see Chapter 7) which deliberately tries to match the S&P 500—it may not be able to outperform the market. Yet, despite positions in many securities—about 1,800 in mid-1987—Magellan Fund has been able to do so over time. Clearly there are no easy guidelines for you to follow. With time and experience, however, you will be able to perceive which funds are diversified too little to guard against industry and company risks and which are diversified too well.

risk in the environment in which you're planning to invest. You may wish to reinforce or update your conclusion by drawing inferences from movements in a fund's NAV on days when the market has moved significantly up or down. If a fund's NAV changed less than the S&P 500 on days of large fluctuations, it's probable that a significant share of the fund's assets is in cash.

Step 5: Asset Size

The final major test to which you should submit a fund is total net assets. A stock fund that is too large may be handicapped in trying to perform well in a rising or falling market.

When buying shares, a fund with billions of dollars in assets cannot easily concentrate its investments among companies of modest size in the most promising industries without driving prices up. Having so much money to invest, it even has to guard against buying control of small companies.

When reducing or liquidating its position in a company, a giant fund also has to be extremely cautious, lest its selling drive the price of the shares down too much.

Because a very large fund has to spread its money among many industries and companies, you generally can expect that its return would tend to be average rather than above-average.

We're looking for above-average returns and, consequently, feel there ought to be some limit to the size of a fund in which you begin your long-term investment program. The figure we suggest—perhaps a bit arbitrarily—is $1 billion of net assets. We'd pass up any fund exceeding $1 billion.

A glance at Table 4-5 will indicate why it's hard to be dogmatic about this or any other criterion. Aside from the extraordinary case of Magellan, you'll note that another five of the 13 largest equity funds ranked in the top 50 for performance in the five years ended in 1986, and three more made the top 100.

On the other hand, the list of the top 10 funds for this period il-

TABLE 4-5. How Giants Have Performed

Fund	Assets as of Dec. 31, 1986 (in Millions)	1982–1986 Performance Rank
Fidelity Magellan	$7,405.5	1
Vanguard Windsor	4,893.8	30
Investment Company of America	3,730.0	46
Templeton World	3,373.8	94
Fidelity Equity-Income	3,360.0	38
Affiliated Fund	3,170.9	88
Pioneer II	3,100.9	206
Fidelity Puritan	2,965.0	43
Dreyfus Fund	2,308.6	325
American Capital Pace	2,221.2	159
American Mutual	2,162.8	75
Fidelity Overseas	2,065.5	*
Twentieth Century Select	2,048.9	49

*Began in 1984—no 5-year record

Note: Table excludes fixed-income funds

Sources: Assets: Lipper Analytical Services, Inc., as they appeared in *Barron's* February 16, 1987; Performance Rank: *Lipper—Mutual Fund Performance Analysis*.

lustrates how unusual it is for the largest funds to show up among the leaders (Table 4-6).

During much of the four years that Magellan grew from $460 million to $7,405 million, its portfolio manager, Peter S. Lynch, was warning that the fund was too big to continue to grow at such a rapid rate. Yet Magellan continued to do just that, ranking first among all funds not only for the 5, but also for the 10 and 15 years ended in 1986.

In suggesting guidelines for you, we're talking about general principles and the laws of averages—not unusual cases. The probability that funds with $1 billion or more would fail to do what Magellan has done was greater than the probability that they would succeed. When

TABLE 4-6. Five-Year Performance and Size

Fund	1982–1986 Performance Rank	Assets as of Dec. 31, 1986 (In Millions)
Fidelity Magellan	1	$7,405.5
Merrill Lynch Pacific	2	419.2
Vanguard Qualified Dividend I	3	175.2
Vanguard World—International Growth	4	443.6
Loomis-Sayles Capital	5	210.1
Prudential-Bache Utility	6	1,517.5
Fidelity Select Financial	7	92.6
BBK International	8	124.0
Putnam International Equities	9	411.4
Fidelity Select Health	10	229.3

Sources: Performance Rank: *Lipper—Mutual Fund Performance Analysis*; Assets: Lipper Analytical Services, Inc., as they appeared in *Barron's* February 16, 1987.

you're planning to build your capital for the long term, you want the odds to be with you.

As you saw in Table 4-4, we give as much weight to the fund manager as to asset allocation and asset size combined. To pass, a fund requires 75 points, as it did in the first screen.

While we might tolerate a fund whose size gives us pause, we are much less tolerant of a portfolio manager who is relatively new to a superbly performing fund. The risks that the fund would slip are simply too great.

RESULTS OF SCREENING

The Three Scenarios

After you've subjected the leading funds to the two screens and have added their points, you face one of three scenarios:

1. One clearly suitable fund has emerged.
2. No fund on the list seems suitable.
3. You have two or more funds to choose from.

One Clear Winner. If one fund survives your test, you may consider yourself fortunate. You're ready to invest. Turn to Timing Your Investment later in this chapter for pointers on how to begin. And remember to monitor the fund closely (see Chapter 6).

No Fund Wins. If no fund survives the test, you can take one of at least two possible steps:

1. You can defer starting your investment program until next quarter's results provide you a new list of leading performers which may include new candidates. In the meantime, you can simply park in a taxable or tax-exempt money market fund the money which you've designated for equity fund investment.
2. Alternatively, you can (a) relax the criteria to qualify one of the top 25 funds which didn't get enough points, or (b) you can go more deeply into the ranks to identify other funds which you can submit to the screens.

If you choose the latter course, the easiest thing to do would be to turn to one of the annual no-load mutual fund guides for data on the top 50 performers for the last 10 and 5 years. Figure 4-2, for example, shows the list of the top 50 for the five years ended in 1986 (including tax-exempts) as it appeared in the AAII's *Guide*. You'll also use the guide to determine the most recent down year returns, as you did for the top 25 funds. The other steps are also identical to those for the top 25.

Choosing from Two or More Funds. If two or more funds meet the criteria, how do you select the one that's right for you—one in which you can invest without worry?

To ensure that your first fund is one that you can feel comfortable

Top 50 Funds: Five-Year Total Return
(1982 through 1986)

Type	Fund	Return (%)
A	Fairmont	206.1
Intl	T. Rowe Price International	199.9
A	Quest for Value	196.8
Bal	Evergreen Total Return	195.8
Intl	Scudder International	191.1
GI	Ivy Growth	181.9
Bal	Lehman Opportunity	181.3
G	Manhattan	180.5
Bal	Fidelity Puritan	177.4
Bal	Loomis-Sayles Mutual	176.7
A	20th Century Select	176.2
Bal	Safeco Income	172.9
GI	American Leaders (Liberty)	172.2
GI	Selected American Shares	170.3
A	SteinRoe Special	169.8
TE	SteinRoe Managed Municipals	168.9
G	Nicholas	167.2
G	North Star Regional	166.0
Bal	Financial Industrial Income	166.0
GI	Dodge & Cox Stock	165.7
Bd	Fidelity High Income	163.2
Bal	Mutual Shares	162.8
G	Lehman Capital	162.4
Bd	Northeast Investors Trust	162.0
Bal	Mutual Qualified Income	161.8
Bal	Vanguard/Wellington	157.4
Bal	Vanguard/Wellesley	157.0
A	Tudor	155.2
Bd	Stratton Monthly Dividend Shares	154.3
TE	Safeco Municipal	151.3
G	Scudder Capital Growth	150.2
TE	Fidelity High-Yield Municipals	150.2
G	Boston Co. Capital Appreciation	148.9
GI	Partners	148.3
GI	Fidelity Fund	144.6
Bal	Axe-Houghton Fund B	143.8
Bal	Dodge & Cox Balanced	143.6
TE	Federated Tax-Free Income (Liberty)	143.5
G	Copley Tax-Managed	143.3
GI	Guardian Mutual	143.1
G	Century Shares Trust	142.3
GI	Founders Mutual	142.2
TE	Vanguard High-Yield Municipal Bond	139.7
TE	Fidelity Municipal	138.9
Bd	Axe-Houghton Income	138.5
GI	Vanguard Index Trust	138.5
TE	Financial Tax-Free Income Shares	138.1
TE	Vanguard Long-Term Municipal Bond	137.5
A	Evergreen	137.3
TE	Dreyfus Tax-Exempt	137.1

Figure 4-2. Top 50 Performers for 5-Year Period by Type. Reprinted with permission from *The Individual Investor's Guide to No-Load Mutual Funds*, sixth edition, published by the American Association of Individual Investors, Chicago. (A = aggressive growth, Bal = balanced, Bd = bond, G = growth, GI = growth & income, Intl = international, TE = tax-exempt)

with, you have to compare the risk levels and potential for gains of the funds which you're considering. You want a fund which has a risk level that's appropriate for you and which, given that level, is likely to offer you the highest potential for gains.

The risk level. To assess the risk level of each fund, check on three indicators:

1. Its total return in the stock market's last down year. Did it have a positive return or, if not, by how much did it lead the S&P 500?
2. The percentage of assets invested in stocks at the time of its most recent quarterly report.
3. The number of companies whose stocks it owns. A fund that's invested in a very small number is apt to be more volatile than a fund which holds the shares of many companies.

Potential for gain. To assess the potential for gain, go back to the most recent quarterly feature on mutual funds in *Barron's* and look for the table headed "The Best and the Worst," which (at this writing) has been listing the 100 best and 100 worst performing funds since June 30, 1982 (Figure 4-3). Although the period does not quite coincide with the start of the bull market in mid-August 1982, it is close enough to indicate which funds have soared the highest in these up years.

See whether your prospects are among the 100 best, and, if so, whether one ranks significantly higher than the other(s). If their rankings were about equal or close to each other, you might pick the one which made the best showing in the most recent down year.

Other considerations. If the candidates seem about equal in every respect, here are some other points for your consideration:
Loads. Since all of your money works for you when you buy a no-load fund, check whether you can buy the funds' shares at their NAV, or whether you'd have to pay sales charges. If so, how much would the loads be?

Although there has seemed to be a trend to low-loads (that is, up

Fund Name	Objective	% Change 7/30/87	Total Net Asset Mil $ 6/30/87	Fund Name	Objective	% Change 7/30/87	Total Net Asset Mil $ 6/30/87
Merrill Lyn Pacific	IF	508.74	482.4	Scudder Capital Grth	G	257.66	545.5
Vanguard Wrld-Intl Gr	IF	405.67	560.1	Sogen International	G	257.36	102.4
Fidelity Magellan Fd	G	389.83	10,842.3	Twentieth Cent Grth	CA	256.80	1,416.4
Putnam Intl Equities	GL	379.24	611.5	Ivy Growth	G	255.41	204.0
BBK International	IF	378.37	109.4	Mutual Benefit Fund	GI	253.44	19.0
Loomis-Sayles Capital	G	357.82	290.3	New Perspective Fd	GL	252.48	1,118.6
T Rowe Price Intl Fund	IF	332.05	1,003.8	Templeton Growth	GL	252.29	1,446.5
Scudder International	IF	328.95	807.4	Cardinal Fund	GI	252.21	130.5
Fidelity Sel Health	H	321.75	399.6	Pennsylvania Mutual	SG	252.05	358.4
Fidelity Destiny I	G	319.22	1,461.5	Keystone International	IF	252.04	161.5
Weingarten Equity	CA	311.73	258.1	Affiliated Fund	GI	251.61	4,004.2
Alliance International	IF	309.49	194.7	Putnam Voyager	CA	251.59	574.4
Alliance Technology	TK	303.41	200.8	Franklin Equity Fund	G	251.33	298.6
Manhattan Fund	CA	302.10	528.0	IDS New Dimensions	G	250.64	728.8
Phoenix Growth	G	294.30	526.7	Investment Co of Amer	GI	250.54	4,578.3
Vanguard-Qual Dvd I	EI	290.40	192.5	Strong Total Return	CA	248.86	899.2
Legg Mason Value Tr	G	289.21	871.1	Tudor Fund	CA	248.84	212.9
Lehman Opportunity	CA	288.66	103.7	Mutual Shares	GI	248.61	1,904.7
Twentieth Cent Select	G	288.57	2,974.8	Hartwell Growth Fd	CA	248.32	26.2
Windsor Fund	GI	285.11	5,996.1	Vanguard Index Trust	GI	248.28	906.3
Guardian Park Avenue	G	284.48	178.5	Oppenheimer Time	CA	248.27	347.5
Phoenix Stock	CA	284.45	127.3	Quest for Value Fund	CA	247.34	110.3
United Intl Growth	IF	284.19	291.6	Investors Research	CA	246.97	88.9
Princor Capital Accum	CA	283.90	93.5	Boston Co Cap Apprec	G	246.57	567.1
New Eng Growth Fund	G	283.76	471.8	Seligman Capital	CA	246.38	234.6
Dodge & Cox Stock	GI	283.60	71.1	Sentinel Common Stock	GI	246.32	604.6
Federated Stock Trust	GI	280.61	749.7	Seligman Com Stock	GI	245.75	633.0
Kemper Int'l Fd	IF	280.50	236.8	Lehman Capital Fund	CA	244.47	120.2
Constellation Growth	CA	280.36	149.0	United Contl Income	B	243.73	383.9
SteinRoe Special Fund	CA	280.12	271.9	Mutual Qualified Inc	GI	243.53	759.8
Oppenheimer Globl Fd	GL	278.02	517.1	Pru-Bache Equity Fd	G	243.25	557.5
Lexington Goldfund	AU	277.72	80.1	Founders Mutual	GI	243.06	227.7
International Investors	AU	277.66	1,132.3	Amev Fiduciary Fd	CA	240.56	36.0
United Income	EI	277.15	1,060.0	Sentinel Growth Fund	G	239.82	65.6
Fairmont Fund	CA	277.11	109.7	Loomis Sayles Mutual	B	238.70	304.7
Fundamental Investors	GI	275.34	691.3	Pilgrim Magnacap	G	238.61	245.7
New York Venture	G	272.33	228.8	American Leaders	GI	238.36	181.1
Merrill Lyn Basic Value	GI	270.99	1,159.0	Selected Amer Shares	GI	238.30	301.7
Templeton Global I	GL	268.81	337.0	Mass Finl Emerg Gro	SG	238.22	317.6
Franklin Gold Fund	AU	268.04	273.9	United Accumulative	G	238.19	821.7
Fidelity Sel Financial	S	267.96	60.3	Shearson Appreciation	G	237.94	514.8
Templeton World	GL	266.08	4,199.0	Nicholas Fund	G	236.81	1,294.2
Nationwide Growth	G	265.78	235.3	Sigma Capital Shares	CA	236.29	98.5
Transatlantic Gwth Fd	IF	263.82	100.9	Dreyfus Leverage Fund	CA	236.09	588.4
Washington Mutual Inv	GI	263.35	2,881.6	Fidelity Equity-Income	EI	234.01	4,178.8
Oppenheimer Equity	EI	263.08	730.1	Decatur I	EI	233.87	1,636.0
FPA Paramount	GI	261.05	134.7	Elfun Trusts	G	232.72	589.8
Fidelity Sel Prec-Mtls	AU	260.05	402.2	Safeco Income Fund	EI	232.63	290.5
Quasar Associates	G	259.64	134.9	Putnam Vista Basic Val	CA	232.38	265.2
Corp Leaders Tr-B	GI	258.15	88.8	Columbia Growth	G	231.95	250.4

Figure 4-3. The 100 Funds That Led the 1980s Bull Market. Source: Lipper Analytical Services, Inc., as it appeared in *Barron's* August 10, 1987. Performance measured from June 30, 1982, shortly before the bull market began, through July 30, 1987. (Investment objectives: AU = gold oriented, B = balanced, CA = capital appreciation, EI = equity-income, G = growth, GI = growth & income, GL = global, H = health, IF = international, S = specialty, SG = small company growth, TK = science & technology)

to 3%), we do not believe that load funds give you something for the extra money that no-loads don't. There may be times when the reward in a load investment fund is proportionately greater, but a look at the data indicates to us—and it will to you—that you can achieve your objectives with no-load funds most of the time.

(Note: When you study total returns for funds in any publication, the data you see are based on NAVs and, thus, they do not reflect loads. Because you'd be paying a higher offering price if you bought a load fund, an investment of a given sum would not grow as much as the NAV increase shown—or as much as an identical investment in a no-load with the same NAV increase.)

Other Charges. You'll also want to know whether you'd be expected to pay redemption fees and/or annual distribution charges (the so-called 12b-1 plan fees) and, if so, how much. It's important to know this ahead of time; these charges add up and can retard your portfolio's performance. Total expenses should not exceed 1.25–1.50% of net assets.

TIMING YOUR INVESTMENT

Success in investing depends in part on buying securities at the lowest cost. Since neither you nor anyone else ever knows whether the price of any share is as low as it's likely to get, a prudent practice is to buy more shares when prices are low and fewer when they are higher.

A systematic, proven way to do this, illustrated in Table 4-7, is dollar-cost averaging. It involves investing fixed amounts at more or less regular intervals until you have reached your objective (or wish to, or must, stop for some other reason).

Mutual fund investing lends itself beautifully to dollar-cost averaging. With the possible exception of initial minimum requirements—which range up to $3,000, with few exceptions, but are perhaps most commonly $1,000—virtually no dollar-cost averaging plan can entail sums too small for a suitable equity fund. And if you're investing in a no-load fund, you're not penalized with proportionately higher sales charges or broker's commissions when you invest small amounts.

TABLE 4-7. How Dollar-Cost Averaging Works

Date of Purchase	Amount of Purchase	Price per Share	Number of Shares
July 24	$ 1,000	$17.11	58.445
Aug. 4	1,000	16.61	60.205
Aug. 15	1,000	17.15	58.309
Aug. 25	1,000	17.15	58.309
Sep. 12	1,000	15.71	63.654
Sep. 24	1,000	16.36	61.125
Oct. 3	1,000	16.24	61.576
Oct. 14	1,000	16.38	61.050
Oct. 21	1,000	16.37	61.087
Nov. 3	1,000	17.06	58.617
Nov. 17	1,000	17.03	58.720
Nov. 28	1,000	17.06	58.617
Total	$12,000	16.67	719.714

This example, which happens to depict twelve purchases of Strong Opportunity Fund in 1986, illustrates how dollar-cost averaging enabled an investor to buy more shares. As shown, $12,000 over time bought 719.714 shares for an average cost of $16.67. If all $12,000 had been invested at the beginning, the investor would have acquired only 701.344 shares and, at $17.06, would have shown a paper loss instead of a modest gain.

To get started with the fund of your choice, you simply have to establish how much you want to invest per year, subtract the required initial minimum, and divide the balance into equal investments that meet the fund's minimum requirements for subsequent installments. If you're committed to stay with dollar-cost averaging, the market can be high or low when you begin; it won't matter in the long run.

If you're approaching the time when the fund is going to declare a dividend or capital gains distribution, wait until the fund's shares are traded "ex distribution." Otherwise, you'd be liable for income tax on a distribution sooner than you'd want. (This is especially applicable to funds that pay distributions annually, thus exposing you to greater tax liability than is the case with quarterly distributions.)

Mutual fund investing that follows the discipline of dollar-cost averaging allows investors to ignore, most of the time, the consequences of dividend or capital gains distributions.

Unless you need or prefer to make a large lump sum payment into a fund to start, we suggest that you begin slowly and keep your initial investments the same. If you have the money, you can increase your periodic investments later when you have more experience and are more familiar with the skills of your fund's management.

In considering how to proceed, you may wish to think of using a money market fund to supplement this scheme. A money market fund will come in handy if your equity fund's minimum initial investment exceeds the cash you have available and you wish to save money from current income until you have enough. Similarly, you can use the money market fund to save between subsequent installments. (Be sure, of course, that such installments would not fall below the minimum amounts for which you are able to write checks on your money market fund.)

While falling stock prices will test your determination—and everybody else's—you'll want to bear in mind that the largest profits can be made when depressed prices let you buy more shares. Similarly, you may think it's crazy to keep buying as the market heads for a peak. Remember that no one ever knows ahead of time when the peak will occur. If your program is well established by then, your continuing purchases merely will raise the average cost of your shares a little.

In either case, be sure to monitor the fund's performance, as discussed in Chapter 6, to guard against surprises.

5

EXPANDING YOUR FUND PORTFOLIO

As you see how well your first equity mutual fund is working out, the time probably will come when you will want to invest in others. We know the feeling. Even when we're doing or thinking about other things, it is reinforced daily by the persuasive promotional messages with which many funds bombard us in newspaper, radio, television, and direct mail advertising.

Having followed the discipline of our selection process, you may feel confident that you can pick a second or third fund exactly the same way. While the key elements of fund selection remain the same, there are, however, additional points to keep in mind. We urge you, therefore, to keep your checkbook closed until you've become familiar with them as well.

131

In this chapter, we'll consider why it might be a good idea to expand your equity fund portfolio, when you might begin to add one or more funds, how to choose the additional fund(s), how many you might invest in, and whether the number ought to be limited.

THE CASE FOR INVESTING IN OTHER FUNDS

If you could find an equity fund that is certain to be the *top* performer *every* year, you obviously would not need to think of investing in any other. You'd invest *all* your money in that fund. Investing in others would reduce your expected return.

Unfortunately, all of us have to assume that no fund will *always* lead in performance. It makes sense, therefore, to consider adding to your first fund when you're ready, and have identified a suitable candidate.

Although your first fund may be living up to your expectations—or, we hope, even exceeding them—you might find it desirable to invest in a second fund for one of at least two reasons:

1. To reduce your exposure to risk.
2. To raise your expected return.

You should be able to achieve either of these objectives by investing in a second fund which passes our screens, but differs in certain characteristics from the first.

Reducing Exposure to Volatility

The screens which you used to find your first fund were intended to make it reasonably certain that a fund with a satisfactory score would be one whose annual rate of return fluctuated relatively little. That is to say, it would expose you to relatively low risk. (For a brief discussion of risk, see box.) In all probability, this describes your first fund very well.

MEASURING RISK AND USING THE MEASURE

Efforts to develop optimum portfolios by measuring, utilizing, and off-setting investment risk have led to the growth of an enormous—and difficult—body of literature in the more than three decades since Dr. Harry M. Markowitz published his classic work on the subject.

Assuming that you do not have the time or interest in mathematical concepts that are as complicated as they are admirable, we have tried to keep matters simple.

One concept, however, may be worth your time: beta. Long applied to common stocks, beta coefficients have become increasingly used to measure the risks inherent in mutual funds. Simply put, a beta coefficient—beta for short—is used to describe the risk level of a fund in terms of the relationship of its fluctuation to that of the stock market as a whole. For this purpose, the S&P 500 index, used to represent the market, is said to have a beta of 1.0. (In contrast, cash, a riskless asset whose nominal value remains constant, has a beta of 0.0).

If, on the average, a fund rises and falls 75% as much as the index, the fund's beta is said to be .75.

If, on the average, a fund rises and falls 25% more than the index, its beta is—you guessed it—1.25.

Note the words "on the average." While we refer elsewhere to making beta-like calculations every week or on very volatile days to sense short-term prospects, a beta measure which is more descriptive of a fund under various conditions needs to reflect its comparative behavior over longer periods. The common period for mutual fund betas, calculated in 1987 by such sources as the American Association of Individual Investors, CDA Investment Technologies, and the *United Mutual Fund Selector*, was 3 years. (It was not 5 years, as is common with reporting services' betas for stocks, because many funds were not yet 5 years old. Nonetheless, *Mutual Fund Values* calculates betas for 5 years for funds that have been in existence that long or longer.)

In building a portfolio, you want maximum return for the level of risk (or volatility)—the beta level, that is—which you wish to incur or a minimum beta for a given level of return.

Thus, when we talk about adding a second fund to reduce risk, we refer to the objective of finding a fund with a lower beta than your first. When we talk of raising your return, we're talking about finding a fund with a higher beta than your first—and, therefore, one that should generate a commensurately higher return. Regrettably, however, there are no guarantees that you'll earn a higher return every time you incur a higher risk. As Table 5-1 illustrates vividly, it's quite possible to find funds with higher betas whose returns are not higher proportionately—or funds with high returns that do not necessarily have high betas.

Understanding such a contrast brings up another mathematical concept, the alpha coefficient. It is used to compare how well a fund performs at given beta levels—that is, by how much better it performs in comparison with the S&P 500 than its beta would lead you to expect. Services, such as CDA, regularly publish alphas along with betas. Even if you do not wish to take the time to scrutinize both data on a regular basis, you ought at minimum to remember that knowing a fund's risk level may not be enough—it's also useful to know how well the fund manages risk. Or, to put it in technical prose, how high its alpha is.

While the numbers look precise and the concepts are plausible and demonstrable, you cannot expect your portfolio always to behave in a totally predictable way in response to your fine tuning its average beta (and alpha).

The most you should expect, if you choose to invoke betas in your assessments, is a general notion of comparable risks among a group of funds so that, in building your portfolio, you'll be more easily able to attain a weighted average risk level that is appropriate for you (see Building with Betas at the end of this chapter).

TABLE 5-1. Risk and Reward Among Top No-Load Funds 1982–86*

Type	Fund	5-Year Return	Beta
A	Fairmont	206.1%	.91
Intl	T. Rowe Price International	199.9	.51
A	Quest for Value	196.8	.66
Bal	Evergreen Total Return	195.8	.59
Intl	Scudder International	191.1	.50
GI	Ivy Growth	181.9	.67
Bal	Lehman Opportunity	181.3	.84
G	Manhattan	180.5	1.08
Bal	Fidelity Puritan**	177.4	.53

Type	Fund	5-Year Return	Beta
Bal	Loomis-Sayles Mutual	176.7	.84
A	20th Century Select	176.2	1.19
Bal	Safeco Income	172.9	.74
GI	American Leaders**	172.2	.59
GI	Selected American Shares	170.3	.68
A	SteinRoe Special	169.8	1.08
G	Nicholas	167.2	.70
G	North Star Regional	166.0	.90
Bal	Financial Industrial Income	166.0	.79
GI	Dodge & Cox Stock	165.7	1.04
Bd	Fidelity High Income	163.2	.29
Bal	Mutual Shares	162.8	.42
G	Lehman Capital**	162.4	1.12
Bd	Northeast Investors Trust	162.0	.20
Bal	Mutual Qualified Income	161.8	.40
Bal	Vanguard/Wellington	157.4	.70
Bal	Vanguard/Wellesley	157.0	.46
A	Tudor	155.2	1.15
Bd	Stratton Monthly Dividend	154.3	.49
G	Scudder Capital Growth	150.2	1.01
G	Boston Company Capital Appreciation	148.9	.90
GI	Partners	148.3	.79
GI	Fidelity Fund	144.6	.95
Bal	Axe-Houghton Fund B	143.8	.71
Bal	Dodge & Cox Balanced	143.6	.74
G	Copley Tax-Managed	143.3	.51
GI	Guardian Mutual	143.1	.86
G	Century Shares Trust	142.3	1.01
GI	Founders Mutual	142.2	1.04
Bd	Axe-Houghton Income	138.5	.32
GI	Vanguard Index Trust	138.5	1.00
A	Evergreen	137.3	.87

A = Aggressive growth, Bal = Balanced, Bd = Bond, G = Growth, GI = Growth and income, Intl = International,
* Excludes tax-exempt funds
** Became load fund in 1987

Source: *The Individual Investor's Guide to No-Load Mutual Funds*, sixth edition, American Association of Individual Investors, Chicago.

Nonetheless, changing circumstances, such as a strong rise in stock prices or growth in assets, might make it prudent to moderate your risk exposure even further by adding another fund to your portfolio. It would not only add to the diversification of your investments; it could also have its assets allocated in such a way that it's less volatile.

Suppose, for example, you've been in a fund that has experienced a 20% increase in a certain period, exceeding the rise of the S&P 500. You find another fund that's only 50% in stocks—the rest in cash and its equivalents—and has increased only 10%. If you had invested an equal amount in the second fund, your total portfolio would have gone up by a 15% in the same period. If the market had fallen instead, your first fund might have dropped 20% and the other one, 10%, causing your total investment to decline 15%. By accepting a lower rate of increase during an advancing market, you would have "paid" for protection against what's called "downside risk."

By investing in a second fund and adjusting the relative sizes of your investments in each, you can influence the level of your portfolio's risk—the degree to which you participate in rising and falling markets.

One of the advantages of reducing the risk level of your portfolio is that it enables you to stay invested, which is usually what you'd want to do—even in a bear market.

Panicking and selling out after experiencing a drop during a market decline—instead of deliberately reducing your holdings when you had planned to—can be enormously costly. It not only can cause you large losses because you'd be selling when prices are low, it also can deprive you of the chance to benefit from the eventual recovery—unless you have a truly rare sense of timing that would lead you to buy back in at the bottom.

If you're like many other investors—professionals as well as amateurs—you might not have the confidence to buy equity fund shares until a bull market is well along. How many investors had the courage to buy stocks when the great bull market of the 1980s began with the Dow Jones Industrial Average at 776.92? How many had it when the

Dow was 100% higher in December 1985? How many still had confidence when the Dow was 200% higher in March 1987?

Superficially, it may not seem sensible to continue investing on a dollar-cost averaging basis and to remain invested when a market is sagging. But perhaps you'll perceive it as prudent if your investment horizon is a long one—allowing time for market recovery—and if you're in a fund that raises its cash position when desirable, is adept at stock selection, or both. By being in a fund that raises and lowers its cash position, you let the experts try to perform a degree of market timing for you without liquidating stocks altogether.

Perhaps you'll be encouraged to remain invested by the Magellan Fund's comment to its shareholders that it had achieved its successful record through 1986 despite its staying fully invested during eight market declines of over 10% in the latest 10 years.

RAISING YOUR RETURN

If your first fund is a conservatively managed, well-diversified fund which is staying on track toward your long-term goal, you may wish to raise your rate of return by investing in a second fund which has been doing better than your first.

While both funds may be very much alike in terms of risk or asset size, or may both have growth as a common investment objective, the manager of the second somehow has produced a better record recently. It could be, for example, that the manager of the first is not following the same discipline that was pursued earlier and the manager's style may have evolved into a more conservative one.

The second fund, too, could be well-diversified among industries and companies, but it might be more inclined to invest in small firms or in large, growing firms that pay lower dividends because they need to reinvest more of their earnings than companies in mature industries. Or the manager of the second fund simply might be better at stock selection. Clearly, there is no one reason for differences in rates of return. Nor is there one manager for all seasons, although a small number have shown remarkable staying power.

In considering your fund selections, remember that market conditions change and that no fund manager has proven an ability to stay on top in all economic environments.

Although for reasons discussed in Chapter 2 we advise against relying too heavily on how any one reporting service classifies funds, we'll see in Chapter 7 how it might be useful to look at Lipper data in *Barron's* to get a sense of which groups are gaining strength.

WHEN THE TIME IS RIGHT

There is no absolute rule for deciding when the time would be right for you to begin investing in a second fund. A number of factors could lead you to such decision. Examples follow.

Money

You are earning enough current income to sustain a dollar-cost averaging program in two funds simultaneously without affecting your standard of living or risking too great a share of your assets.

How much money would you need to start investing in a second fund? There are no firm rules. You might think of investing in a second fund if you're able to invest at a rate of more than $250 a month—$3,000 a year—in the two funds combined. Funds' minimum investment requirements are low enough, on the average, to make this feasible. (If you can invest more than $500 a month, or $6,000 a year, you could think in terms of three funds.)

Comfort Level

After you have been investing in the first fund for several months, you should feel comfortable placing your money at risk in investments generally and in mutual funds in particular. Presumably you will have begun to understand the dynamics of investing and have adjusted to the experience.

If your first investment coincided with a drop in the market, your understanding will have been more important and your adjustment more difficult. In a rising market, adjustment will have been deceptively easier. The relatively minor "corrections" which occur during a bull market do not really prepare anyone for the plunges of a bear market that can take your breath away. Beta readings on bad down days, however, can be useful in indicating your risks for the longer term. Even a bull market is no time to ease up on trying to understand what's happening so that you fully discern why you should feel at ease with your investments.

Free Time

You have adequate free time to manage your money. As you will see in the next chapter, a modest amount of time is required to monitor a fund weekly—plus an additional amount quarterly—to decide whether any action is necessary and, if so, to take that action. Doubling the number of funds would approximately double the time you'd need. Monitoring and managing your portfolio are so essential that you ought not to invest in more funds than you have time for every weekend.

Market Cycle

If you will be investing in a second fund by dollar-cost averaging over a long period, your timing will be much less important.

When the market is down and may even be going lower, the time may be especially opportune because you can acquire more of a fund's shares for a given amount of money. It takes a bit of nerve and confidence in what you're doing, but you should make out all right if you stay with your program at least through the decline and the market's next peak, whenever that may be.

If the market is ascending, you need not defer investing in a second fund—especially if the second fund is not fully rising with the market, an indication that it may do relatively better eventually when the market turns down. Neither you nor anyone else can know when the peak will occur, and you might wait a long time. (How many warned against buying stocks as the Dow Jones Industrial Average approached, and then exceeded, 2000 because the market was "too high"?)

Simply take precautions (aside from the obvious one of not investing an excessive share of your assets in stocks): Find a less volatile fund and stretch your dollar-cost averaging program by investing smaller amounts over a longer period.

Since you've embarked on a long-term program, remember to keep a long-term perspective: In the long run, equities should outperform other financial assets and protect you against inflation, as we saw in Chapter 1.

Age

You're only as old as you feel, they say, and this is true in many respects. But when it comes to investments, age becomes a more absolute—if not totally fixed—concept. Unavoidably, your age has to be a key factor in your investment planning.

Given the importance of staying with equity investments long enough to enjoy the rewards of a rising market, you will only want to begin buying into an additional fund if you are not likely to retire or otherwise need your money before the market hits its next peak.

Since stock market cycles vary significantly in length (Chapter 1), you should take a look at economic and market conditions, and make an educated guess as to whether the ingredients for a peak are present or mounting. Stocks turn down for several reasons, such as an expected or actual plunge in corporate profits or an expected or actual rise in interest rates.

In the absence of fixed rules as to how much profits must slip or rates must rise for equities to begin to fall, it is not easy for anyone— professional or amateur—to predict the next peak.

You simply do the best you can. If you keep up generally with what's happening in stock and bond markets and the rest of the economy, your estimate may be as good as anyone else's. Moreover, you can always change it as new data comes out.

The main thing is that, if you're in your mid-50s or older, you integrate the notion of a market peak into your planning. Instead of thinking of undertaking additional equity investments, it would be more appropriate for you to begin gradual withdrawal from equity funds when you come within a few years of 65 (unless you're planning to retire earlier or to work beyond 65).

Because retirement is such an individual matter, we can't really offer very much, but we do make one suggestion: Even though you may have a good idea of when you'd prefer to retire—and may be directing your investment program with this in mind—be prepared to change your investment strategy suddenly. As so many have already done in the 1980s, your employer could surprise you with an early retirement offer that would be hard—if not impossible—to turn down.

CHOOSING ADDITIONAL FUNDS

In considering a second fund, you will want to look for another superior performer that passes our screens, but that complements the first, instead of imitating or even resembling it.

Ideally, the second fund would be likely to rise and fall at different rates or times, to invest in companies of different sizes, to have a different orientation that persuades it to give greater weight to other industries, or to regard holding cash more (or less) favorably.

Going for Growth

It is quite likely that you first chose a fund that is primarily invested in high-yield stocks and fixed-income securities because you wanted to proceed cautiously. As you see the stock market advancing at a faster pace than your fund, and you want to participate in the action, you could begin to invest in a fund which is primarily committed to seeking capital gains.

Using our selection procedure, develop a list of prospects. Then get their prospectuses and see which ones give growth as their only objective. Pick the one with the best record over a period of years—the one most likely to help you to attain *your* objective. It probably will be one that's fully invested in stocks—predominantly shares of companies with prospects for the fastest growth in profits. While such a fund would be inherently risky, you could afford to be in it because of the solid foundation your first fund provides your portfolio.

You may wish to get into a small company fund if a suitable one emerges from your analysis. When people question whether a market rise is real, they feel more secure owning shares of large corporations, which pay dividends that are high in relation to their earnings and the prices of their shares. Funds that are heavily invested in such shares tend to do better during such periods.

As individual and institutional investors bid up shares of large companies, shares of worthy small companies, which have been overlooked, are apt to be perceived as better values, and funds owning them will make a better showing. Most likely, these will be funds that are still small enough to be able to buy such shares without unduly driving up their prices.

Capital Preservation

If your first fund is a growth fund that performs well, but you now want to give safety of principal a higher priority, you will want a second fund whose portfolio will serve that objective. It'll probably turn out to be a fund investing in larger companies which pay high dividends and have strong balance sheets, or one that has achieved an impressive return despite having 25% or more of its assets in cash. By investing sufficiently in such a fund, you should be able to relax about retaining the first one to earn capital gains.

You can get an idea of how well a fund might preserve your capital by studying its market behavior before investing. Look for one whose share price moves about 50% as much as the S&P 500 on a day when the stock market moves down strongly.

Capital Gains vs. Income

In eliminating preferential federal income tax treatment of long-term capital gains, the Tax Reform Act of 1986 put long- and short-term capital gains and current income on the same basis.

Although identical tax rates now should leave you indifferent as to whether you are taxed on a dividend or capital gains distribution, you may prefer a second fund that gives current income a higher priority than capital gains—or one that does the opposite.

The dividend portion of a fund's total return tends to be more stable than the combination of realized and unrealized capital gains. Thus, if you require more stability or must depend on cash from a certain level of distribution, instead of reinvesting it in more shares, you probably should consider a fund which makes income—and its growth—a primary objective. Of course, you must be prepared to pay the taxes (unless the fund is in an IRA).

If capital appreciation is more important to you than current income, you might be better off with a fund that tends to hold stocks longer before selling them. Such a fund, identifiable by a relatively low portfolio turnover, exposes you to less of a tax burden (as well as lower brokerage commissions) because it realizes, and distributes, less of its capital gains. For illustration, see Figure 5-1. The risk in such a policy, of course, is that unrealized gains could evaporate. It's a risk that your fund's portfolio manager can, and presumably will, deal with. (If you should suffer capital losses, remember that they still can be offset against capital gains and, up to a limit, against current income.)

Study the prospectuses and reports of the funds you're considering to see how they have phrased their investment objectives, and then check the financial statements to see if they have lived up to their stated policies. It's not enough to go by the commonly used labels, such as growth or growth and income. They are not uniformly applied (see Chapter 2) and can be confusing.

The foregoing points can be illustrated simply by looking at data for two funds in the Vanguard group: Wellesley Income Fund, whose stated objective is "seeking as much current income as in manage-

Statement of Net Assets (Continued)
March 31, 1987

	Shares or Principal Amount	Cost (Note 1(a))	Quoted Market Value (Note 1(a))
COMMON STOCKS — 66.0% (Continued)			
Insurance — 7.9% (Continued)			
The Hanover Insurance Company	50,000	$ 780,625	$ 3,637,500
Torchmark Corporation	307,900	8,582,021	9,121,538
		86,343,358	102,436,383
Printing and Publishing — 1.7%			
Meredith Corporation	270,000	6,098,460	9,585,000
Postal Instant Press +	251,400	3,090,388	4,053,825
Times Mirror	107,400	7,967,792	8,954,475
		17,156,640	22,593,300
Real Estate — 1.1%			
Americana Hotels & Realty*	91,000	964,022	1,080,625
Lomas & Nettleton Financial Corporation	112,500	1,669,515	4,106,250
Lomas & Nettleton Mortgage Investors	340,000	8,268,563	8,712,500
		10,902,100	13,899,375
Retail Trade — 3.9%			
Dillard Department Stores	350,000	10,678,994	14,656,250
Dollar General Corporation	30,000	423,750	322,500
May Department Stores Company	280,000	10,477,125	12,880,000
Pic'N' Save Corporation*	521,750	2,550,010	14,543,780
Rose's Stores, Inc. — Class A	90,000	1,059,687	1,845,000
Rose's Stores, Inc. — Class B	318,000	3,503,875	6,916,500
		28,693,441	51,164,030
Transportation — 1.2%			
Laidlaw Transportation Limited — Class B	600,000	2,061,495	12,300,000
P.S. Group	92,400	3,411,054	3,407,250
		5,472,549	15,707,250
Utilities — 3.6%			
American Water Works Company, Inc.	100,000	1,982,229	4,587,500
Centerior Energy Corporation	158,600	3,260,222	3,568,500
Consumers Power Company*	150,000	1,812,000	2,775,000
Gulf States Utilities	750,000	6,312,413	6,468,750
Long Island Lighting Company*	1,600,000	17,745,458	17,400,000
Northern Indiana Public Service Company*	280,000	3,052,250	3,220,000
Public Service Company of Indiana, Inc.*	300,000	3,711,142	4,875,000
Southwest Gas Corporation	126,100	2,246,969	3,341,650
		40,122,683	46,236,400
Miscellaneous — 5.1%			
Canadian Marconi Company	320,000	3,676,365	5,120,000
Capital Cities ABC Inc.	25,000	5,800,702	8,562,500
DeBeers Consolidated Mines, Ltd.	2,250,000	16,377,433	29,531,250
Laidlaw Industries, Inc.	392,000	3,699,513	9,212,000
Pansophic Systems	51,000	1,361,080	1,836,000
Sonesta International Hotels Corporation — Class A	148,500	1,507,875	2,598,750
Spectra-Physics, Inc.*	250,000	5,310,803	5,468,750
FCA International Ltd.	240,000	1,529,333	3,518,640
		39,263,104	65,847,890
TOTAL COMMON STOCKS		606,809,604	857,391,041

Figure 5-1. Unrealized Appreciation Can Add Up. This excerpt from the Nicholas Fund annual report for the year ended March 31, 1987, illustrates how a fund with a low (27%) yearly portfolio turnover rate can accumulate $250 million in unrealized appreciation on common stocks that cost $607 million.

ment's judgment is consistent with reasonable risk," and Windsor II, which "seeks long-term growth of capital and income" and whose "secondary objective is to endeavor to provide current income." (See Table 5-2.)

In Wellesley's case, current income accounted for slightly more than half of its increase in net assets resulting from operations while capital gains accounted for three-fourths of Windsor II's increase. And of that, unrealized gains exceeded realized gains by a considerable margin. (These examples, taken only from 1986, may or may not be indicative of what the two funds will do in the future.)

Spotting New Trends

You should check the latest—or next—*Barron's* mutual funds issue for newcomers to the list of the top 25 performers for the last 5 years. Screen them for the criteria which your first fund had to pass.

It's possible that a newcomer may have just been in business for 5 years—that it was formed to capitalize on a change in the economy or some new investment opportunities, and that it has succeeded. If the fund is too new to have a 10-year record—or to have experienced a down year—you may wish nonetheless to consider adding it to your

TABLE 5-2. Shares of Increase in Net Assets Resulting from Operations (for Fiscal Years Ended in 1986)

Fund	Net Investment Income	Realized Net Gains	Increase in Unrealized Appreciation
Wellesley Income	52.4%	26.6%	21.0%
Windsor II	21.9	30.6	47.4

Source: The Vanguard Group of Investment Companies
Note: Totals do not necessarily add due to rounding.

portfolio if it passes on other counts. If it's really riding a new trend, it could turn out to be a very good investment.

If a fund is a sector fund—one that's essentially invested in only one industry, for example—it may be too risky for you, but it may give you a clue to another fund: a diversified fund that is heavily invested in the particular sector. Finding such a fund may require some digging in directories.

Family's New Offspring

Clones. You may wish to relax the constraints of our screens in order to consider investing in the "clone" of a successful fund which has met most, if not all, of our criteria.

Mutual fund management companies with popular, successful growth funds, sometimes form clones when they want to market new aggressive growth or growth funds whose sales could benefit from the popularity of the older ones. They even may have closed the parent funds to new investors because the funds had become too large to manage.

Clones may, or may not, be managed by the same people who managed the portfolios of the successful parent funds. They tend to be more volatile and perform poorly in weak markets because, being smaller, they take fewer positions and may be invested in smaller companies.

Fidelity, Heine Securities, Lindner, Nicholas, Quest Advisory, and Vanguard are some of the organizations which have introduced clones.

Since you are likely to hear increasingly about clones, and since clones may be expected to outperform their parents, it's important for you to know how to look at one.

First, find out who manages the clone. If he or she is an understudy of the parent's manager, and if the investment objectives are similar to those of the parent, you have a good bet. If it's the same person, you have a better bet. In some cases—for example, Vanguard's Windsor I and Windsor II—parent and clone have separate, unrelated investment advisers. In such cases, you'll want to learn what you can about the clone's manager, not only by reading the prospectus, but also by checking the other funds that he or she has been managing.

Second, determine how many shares the directors own, if you can. If they own significant numbers, it's an encouraging sign if not a guarantee of the fund's success—at least you know the insiders are risking some of their own money.

Otherwise, you'll want to check the same points that you've applied to other funds: relative price movements on days when the market is volatile, asset allocation to see whether the manager is doing well even though not fully invested in stocks, and diversification among industries and companies. Stay away if a fund drops by a bigger percentage than the S&P 500 on a day when the market falls sharply and doesn't compensate for it on an up day.

If you've satisfied yourself after phoning, studying, and watching the clone, you should be assured and can begin to invest.

Other Siblings. There will be occasions when a fund family that you have learned to respect sponsors a new fund that can be worth looking at. The new family member may—or may not—have totally different investment objectives from its siblings.

Take Strong Opportunity Fund, an aggressive growth fund, for example. Given the showing over several years by older, conservative Strong funds (Strong Total Return and Strong Investment), it could have been regarded as a good candidate for investment *before* it made the list of the top 25 in its first year, 1986. If you had checked out the other Strong funds and studied the Opportunity Fund in the manner suggested for clones, you would have been correct in starting to invest in it, slowly.

Of course, before making such a move you would have wanted to decide whether an aggressive growth fund belonged in your portfolio. If you had none, an aggressive growth fund could have been warranted. If you already owned shares of one or perhaps two aggressive growth funds, and if they were performing satisfactorily, you probably should have passed up the additional risk exposure inherent in Strong Opportunity—member of a respected family or not.

Or consider the case of Fidelity Growth & Income Portfolio. When the large Fidelity organization announced this fund at the start of 1986, it characterized this new offspring as "less 'aggressive' than Fidelity's Growth Funds (but) not as 'conservative' as other Fidelity Growth plus Income Funds," of which there were three: Fidelity Fund, Equity-Income, and Puritan. What was to make the new fund less conservative was a higher asset allocation to stocks.

If one would have determined Fidelity's record in growth and income funds and learned that the new fund's portfolio manager, Elizabeth Terrana, had been an understudy to Bruce Johnstone, the long-time manager of the Equity-Income Fund, one might have invested—and been pleasantly surprised. In only its first seven months, the fund had a return of over 32%. At more than double the return of the S&P 500, it was an unexpectedly hot pace for this type of fund and was not expected to be sustainable. In ensuing quarters the fund rose and fell less than the S&P 500—a performance more characteristic of growth and income funds generally—but still impressive for its category.

HOW MANY FUNDS

The question of how many equity mutual funds would constitute a model, or even a suggested, portfolio really becomes two questions:

How many funds can you afford and manage?

How many funds does it take to achieve your goal(s)?

Money, Time, and Peace of Mind

You know better than anyone else how much money you can invest and how much time you can devote to selecting funds and managing your fund portfolio.

The minimum amount of money you can invest in a year of dollar-cost averaging has little bearing on the number of funds whose shares you can buy. That's because the funds' minimum investment requirements tend to be small, and you can adjust the frequency of your investments to accommodate your cash inflow.

A more important financial constraint is the maximum percentage of your total financial assets which you can afford to invest in equity mutual funds. You don't want to invest money that you cannot afford to lose.

Bearing in mind your funds' cash positions or betas, imagine how a stock market decline of 30% might affect them, and limit your equity position to a figure that will let you sleep at night. This may indicate the number of funds that would be right. (Cash data are especially important guides to volatility in that they reflect the funds' capability to handle redemptions when emotion drives markets and leads to panic selling.)

A sound long-range plan, based on two or more funds whose volatility measures differ, should enable you to stay invested through a market decline and into the eventual recovery; you should not have to sell when prices are depressed in order to pay bills.

The minimum amount of time to monitor and manage may be a more limiting factor. Once each week you should monitor each of your funds to see if one shows signs of underperformance—or is doing so well that profittaking may be timely. To take stock of your portfolio, consider whether any action is required, and act all take time—time that increases in direct proportion to the number of your funds. There are no short cuts. If you find that you do not have the time that is necessary, cut back on the number of funds you're contemplating or already invested in.

Achieving Your Goal(s)

To help ensure that your portfolio will achieve your goal(s), it should consist of enough funds to give you a balance between downside protection and upside potential. Sounds good. But into how many funds do you convert this axiom? Probably no more than three or four (other than a money market fund in which to park cash). You'd combine one or more funds stressing growth with one or more stressing income and, possibly, one giving equal weight to both. The weighting would depend on your circumstances and goals.

Phrased differently, the blend could include a fund that's fully invested in stocks which pay low or no dividends, one that's fully invested in stocks paying high dividends, one that's principally in stocks but has as much as 20% of assets in cash, and perhaps one that owns bonds as well as stocks. (In your major category you might consider one large and one smaller fund since large ones generally do better in down markets and small ones are more likely to excel in up markets.) If market conditions indicate it would make sense, you might add or substitute a fund dedicated to small companies, non-U.S. companies, or precious metals. Each would play a part in helping you to realize your objectives. If a fund did not differ from the others in size, investment objective, or risk level, it would be redundant.

You'd make the selections, using the screens, and adjust the proportions to your own specific requirements. You would not need any more. Given that there are few consistently outstanding fund managers, additional funds would add to your workload without giving you commensurate benefits and might make it difficult for you to remember the role that each was to play in your portfolio. Thus, you'd probably have too many to be able to implement your strategy successfully.

Alternatively, you could assess the risk level—the beta, if you please—which a portfolio for someone in your circumstances should have (see next section). Then, after determining the betas of the funds you own—or are considering—figure how many you might need to get the right mix (or weighted average).

In this case, too, that might be no more than three or four (plus a money market fund): a high beta fund for upside potential, a low beta fund for downside protection, and one or two in between. The money market fund would help to offset the high beta fund, as well as to provide your money a temporary home.

In the case of portfolio construction, too, trial and error will be your best guide since investment strategy has to be based on probabilities in a world of uncertainty. If your portfolio's performance is inadequate or if it fluctuates too much for comfort, you clearly will want to analyze your situation. Intuition may serve you well, but only a rigorous assessment will give you a good idea as to whether expansion, contraction, or merely a shift is called for.

BUILDING WITH BETAS

Two very simple examples will illustrate how fund portfolios can be built by using betas.

If your circumstances indicate that you can tolerate a risk equivalent to that of the market as a whole—that is, if you can tolerate a portfolio with a beta of 1.0—you might divide your portfolio this way: Put 60% into an aggressive growth fund with an assumed beta of 1.3, 30% into a more conservative fund with a beta of .7, and the remaining 10% into a money market fund. This mix would give the portfolio a weighted average of about 1.0, calculated like this:

Fund Type	Portfolio Share	Beta	Beta Weight
Aggressive growth fund	60%	1.3	.78
Conservative fund	30	.7	.21
Money market fund	10	.0	.00
Total portfolio	100%	—	.99

If you had to limit your portfolio's beta to .8, you could use the same funds—but in different proportions:

Fund Type	Portfolio Share	Beta	Beta Weight
Aggressive growth fund	40%	1.3	.52
Conservative fund	40	.7	.28
Money market fund	20	.0	.00
Total portfolio	100%	—	.80

6

MANAGING YOUR MUTUAL FUND PORTFOLIO: TACTICS AND STRATEGIES

After investing in the equity mutual funds which seem most likely to help you to reach your long-term financial goals, you can't just forget about them until the time comes to convert them back into cash. You have to monitor and manage your portfolio to be sure it stays on track.

In this chapter, we will show you how to monitor and manage your funds in a way that takes relatively little of your time. It involves making weekly and quarterly

153

checks of performance, as well as being alert to information about significant developments which may appear anytime in fund mailings and periodicals (Table 6-1).

Our objective is to help you to realize your own long-term goals. This is only possible if you manage your portfolio at a level of risk that you can tolerate. As we noted earlier, you can tolerate a higher volatility in your portfolio's rate of return if you have a long-term horizon than if you don't.

We urge you to watch for signs of possible losses and act early, when necessary, while they're still small. Beginning quickly to redeem your shares in a disappointing fund should enable you to get more of your money out before other investors, rushing to redeem theirs, force the fund to liquidate holdings already under great pressure.

A weekly assessment usually will suffice to keep you current on funds which pass our screens, allowing you to concentrate on your job during working hours—and to sleep at night. It tells you whether your funds' shares are moving within the range you had expected: up with the market during an advance, but falling less than the market during a decline.

Every three months, various quarterly data become available, including new performance statistics for 5- and 10-year periods. You should use these data to analyze your holdings and consider whether any changes seem to be in order.

In brief, we will cover what you should be looking for and how to interpret and act on what you've learned. Most of the time, as you'll see, no action will be called for.

THE IMPORTANCE OF MONITORING

You have the benefit of more safeguards when you invest in well-managed equity mutual funds than when you invest in individual stocks. Yet even funds which have been consistently superior per-

TABLE 6-1. Monitoring: What, When, Where

What to Monitor	When	Where
Individual fund performance	Weekly	*Barron's* or Sunday newspaper
Individual fund performance	Quarterly	Fund report or *Barron's*
Managerial change	Any time	Newspapers or newsletters
Allocation of assets	Quarterly or semi-annually	Fund reports or data services
Size of assets	Quarterly	Fund reports or *Barron's*
Change in objectives or policies	Any time	Fund notices or newsletters
Cost increases	Any time	Fund notices or reports

formers over several years, and which seem to entail only moderate risk, have to be watched.

This is made clear in Table 6-2, which shows the funds that were the top 25 performers for 5-year periods ended in 1982 through 1986, according to Lipper.

Note how few leaders stayed on top, how far some fell, and how none of those dropping out came back within the years shown. Only three of the 1978–1982 leaders were still among the top 25 for 1982–1986.

In the following pages, we will suggest how you can learn to discern deteriorating performance, such as experienced by some of the 1978–1982 leaders, and get out in time in anticipation of a fall. The secret to building your capital over time, remember, is to remain ever alert to the risks of losing it along the way.

It will not surprise you that the principal aspects of your funds that we urge you to watch are those which constitute our screens: fund performance, changes in portfolio managers, asset allocation policies, and fund size. You also will be looking out for changes in fund investment objectives and policies, increases in costs to you, and decisions to close funds to new investors.

PERFORMANCE

Weekly Monitoring

As soon as you have bought shares in your first equity mutual fund, you should develop the habit of assessing weekly changes in its net asset value (NAV) per share. (If you only have time for monitoring once a quarter, stick to low-beta funds.) You may wish to look at your newspaper every morning to see how your fund did the previous day, but it should not be necessary for you to do so.

Finding the Data. In your favorite Sunday newspaper—or *Barron's,* if your paper's coverage of mutual funds is inadequate—you

TABLE 6-2. Rankings of Top 25 Funds for Five-Year Periods Ended 1982–1986

Fund	1978–1982	1979–1983	1980–1984	1981–1985	1982–1986	1982–1986 Other Rank
American Capital Comstock	25	21	*	*	*	202
American Capital Growth	10	*	*	*	*	461
American Capital Pace	7	6	7	*	*	159
American Capital Venture	14	22	*	*	*	383
AMEV Capital	*	*	19	*	*	70
AMEV Growth	13	18	*	*	*	135
BBK International	*	*	*	*	8	
Century Shares Trust	*	*	*	16	*	150
Constellation Growth	23	*	*	*	*	346
Eaton Vance Total Return	*	*	*	*	13	
Evergreen	24	*	*	*	*	172
Evergreen Total Return	*	*	20	15	19	
Fairmont	*	*	*	*	15	
Fidelity Destiny I	*	*	22	12	16	
Fidelity Equity-Income	*	*	12	18	*	38
Fidelity Magellan	4	3	1	3	1	
Fidelity Select Financial	*	*	*	*	7	
Fidelity Select Health	*	*	*	*	10	
Franklin Gold	5	5	*	*	*	480
Franklin Utilities	*	*	*	11	*	40

TABLE 6-2. Continued

Fund	1978–1982	1979–1983	1980–1984	1981–1985	1982–1986	1982–1986 Other Rank
Fund of America	*	*	24	*	*	147
Hartwell Leverage	19	19	*	*	*	348
IDS Growth	12	14	*	*	*	61
Income Fund of America	*	*	*	20	*	444
International Investors	3	4	*	*	*	52
Investors Research	*	*	21	*	*	35
Ivy Growth	*	*	18	25	*	212
Janus	*	*	17	*	*	487
Keystone Precious Metals	*	12	*	*	*	92
Lehman Capital	17	7	11	17	*	37
Lehman Opportunity	*	*	25	8	*	152
Lindner	22	25	3	8	14	
Lindner Dividend	*	*	2	5	5	
Loomis-Sayles Capital	11	15	10	7	5	
Massachusetts Capital Development	15	8	*	*	*	311
Merrill Lynch Pacific	*	*	*	*	2	
Mutual Qualified Income	*	*	*	10	*	73
NEL Growth	8	16	9	23	24	

Fund						
Neuberger & Berman Hemisphere	*	*	*	24	a	
Nicholas	*	*	13	22	*	65
Oppenheimer Directors	*	24	*	*	*	417
Oppenheimer Target	*	*	*	2	*	86
Phoenix Growth	*	*	6	14	11	
Phoenix Stock	*	10	5	19	20	
Price (T.Rowe) International	*	*	*	*	17	
Prudential-Bache Utilities	*	*	*	*	6	
Putnam International	*	*	*	*	9	
Quasar Associates	16	9	*	*	*	124
Quest for Value	*	*	15	4	23	32
Sequoia	*	*	*	6	*	494
Strategic Investments	1	2	*	*	*	
Strong Investment	*	*	*	*	22	
Strong Total Return	*	*	16	*	12	
Tudor	*	20	*	*	*	107
Twentieth Century Growth	6	17	23	*	*	372
Twentieth Century Select	9	11	*	*	25	49
United Continental Income	*	*	*	*	18	
United Income	*	*	*	*	*	
United Services Gold	2	1	8	*	*	488
United Vanguard	18	13	*	*	*	140
Vanguard Explorer	20	*	*	*	*	468
Vanguard Gemini	*	*	*	13	b	

TABLE 6-2. Continued

Fund	1978–1982	1979–1983	1980–1984	1981–1985	1982–1986	1982–1986 Other Rank
Vanguard Qualified Dividend I	*	*	4	1	3	
Vanguard Windsor	*	*	14	9	*	30
Vanguard World—International Growth	*	*	*ᵇ	*	4	
Washington Mutual	*	*	*	21	21	
Weingarten Equity	21	23	*	*	*	68

* = Not among top 25
ᵃ Neuberger & Berman Hemisphere merged into Manhattan, 1986
ᵇ Vanguard Gemini merged into Windsor, 1986
Source: Lipper Analytical Services, Inc. *Lipper—Mutual Fund Performance Analysis.*

first find your fund's closing NAV and change for the week and calculate the percentage by which it rose or fell from the preceding
week's close.

You then should compare the fund's performance with the market
as a whole. You do this by calculating the ratio of its percentage of
increase or decrease to that of the S&P 500 index—a weekly beta
reading. After you buy shares in one or more additional funds and
calculate weekly changes and betas for all, you'll be able to see how
they rank vis à vis one another. (Such a ranking will help you in considering any changes you may wish to make in your allocation of new
money among your funds.)

One to four times a year, calculating your funds' weekly data becomes a bit tricky. When a fund declares a dividend and/or a distribution of capital gains to all who held shares on a stated "record day,"
the NAVs published the following weekend will have been reduced
by the total of the declarations. That's because all who buy shares
after the record day are not entitled to the distributions. To figure
out the rate of return for such a week, you add back the amount of
the declarations to the week's closing NAV.

What often makes this simple task time-consuming is determining
whether a distribution was declared and, if so, what its size is. Newspapers usually alert you to such declarations by inserting an "x" next
to a fund's NAV to indicate it's selling "ex-dividend" or a "d" to indicate it's selling "ex-distribution." If you didn't catch the declarations
in a daily paper, you have to call the fund to get the amounts because
Sunday newspapers don't carry them, and even *Barron's,* complete
as it is, may lag in publishing the information.

Sometimes, however, the papers fail to print the "x" or "d," and
you may inadvertently calculate an incorrect weekly change. If the
distribution is small and the NAV moved in the same direction as the
market, you may not notice the omitted symbol. If, on the other
hand, a fund's NAV is down significantly while the market is up, you
may suspect that a declaration has been made but not indicated.
Check with the fund. (If you are familiar with its declaration schedule,
usually cited in the prospectus, you will know when to expect one.)

If weekly monitoring is too much trouble for you, but quarterly monitoring too infrequent, you might subscribe to newsletters or data services which report fund performance data monthly (reflecting reinvestment of distributions) and facilitate comparisons with fund groups and with the S&P 500. They may be helpful in alerting you to possible losses. (While we are not impressed, on the whole, by their purchase recommendations, they do contain other useful information. Why not get samples of several to see which, if any, you find useful? One subscription should suffice.)

Interpreting and Acting on the Data. The primary objective of weekly data analysis is to help you to preserve your capital by alerting you to the possible, if not actual, decline in the value of your fund holdings. For this purpose, the percentage of change calculation is most important.

Much of the time, your funds—and the market as a whole—will fluctuate in a more or less predictable range. Reassured that nothing noteworthy has occurred and that you don't have to consider taking any action, you can put away your calculator and do something else.

When something unpredictable happens, on the other hand, you may have to do some sharp pencil work and prepare to act.

In the unlikely—but not impossible—event that a fund drops 5% in one week, it's imperative that you check the performance for the following week. If it is off by 5% again and if its drop exceeds that of the S&P 500, stop putting new money into the fund. Its shares may be cheaper, but something may be wrong with the fund's portfolio management or with investors' perception of the fund's group.

If the fund continues dropping a third week, begin to redeem shares. In all likelihood, you're not the only one to have noticed the drop. A selling panic may be under way, feeding on itself, and, therefore, you don't want to delay.

The rate at which you redeem depends on the share of your total assets that the fund represents. If it's a high share, prudence would call for faster redemption. It occasionally happens, as was the case with 44 Wall Street and Hartwell Leverage Fund in 1984, that a fund can fall over 30% in a year (44 Wall's *negative* rate of return actually was about double that). If such a fund constitutes one-half of your holdings, you have a greater need to get out quickly than if it constitutes, say, one-tenth. (For that matter, if a fund constitutes a high share of your assets and you cannot afford to take significant risks, you should consider redemption following consecutive weekly drops in NAV of 3%.)

There is, of course, the possibility that a fund will snap back and that you will have sold too soon. But, remembering the importance of stopping losses early, that's a chance you should probably take. If it eventually turns out that the fund continued sliding, you'll see that you will have been better off parking the money in a money market fund and selecting a new fund the next time Lipper's quarterly data are available.

Funds that perform superbly in an advancing market often, but not always, do so because they take more than normal risks. Such strategy might not work during a declining market and, ironically, could put you at a greater risk.

Most weeks, when the percentage of change in the stock market is small, weekly betas* give you inconclusive clues to your funds' volatility. Don't be surprised if one of your funds even moves in a direction opposite to that of the S&P 500, thereby providing no meaningful beta at all. But if you spot a fund's beta exceeding 1.0 in an up week and falling below 1.0 in a down week, you're watching a skilled manager at work.

While many funds adhere pretty well to strategies that cause their betas to remain essentially constant, others don't. They should be followed more closely, especially during volatile periods. That goes double for funds that, having reserved the right to change asset allocation significantly, may move from fully invested positions to a high

---

*Published betas to help you in fund selection and portfolio planning, based on performance during at least the most recent 36 months, were available annually at this writing in *The Individual Investor's Guide to No-Load Mutual Funds*, semiannually in *United Mutual Fund Selector*, and quarterly in *CDA Mutual Fund Report* and *Mutual Fund Values*.

percentage of cash or the other way around—or from equities to bonds and cash.

Weekly beta readings can serve essentially two purposes. They can constitute a sort of early warning system to alert you when a fund may be beginning a decline or is otherwise falling short of your expectations. They also may tip you when one of your funds is exceeding expectations and may be worth investing in more heavily in the hope of raising your return. Of the two, of course, the defensive use is by far more important.

If you have the time, you also may wish to calculate betas for volatile *days*; a succession of beta readings for several days on which the S&P 500 rises or falls by around 2% or more can be used to project fund performance during a volatile period.

During a down market, you'll especially want to keep your eyes open. If one of your funds has beta readings of 1.0 or more for three or four weeks—that is, if it's performing as badly as, or worse than, the market—and is not making up the slippage during intervening weeks of gains, you may have cause for concern. It isn't only that the fund has been losing value. More important, the signs may point to more substantial decline ahead.

You should stop investing new money in the fund. Do not begin to redeem shares, however, until you have an opportunity to see whether the fund remains among the leaders for 1-, 5-, or 10-year performance, as well as for trough-to-peak gains, in the next quarterly Lipper data. It's possible that the fund did exceedingly well in the year just past, is giving back a part of its gains, and you really should not be concerned.

Just because a fund has been dropping for a few weeks does not automatically mean that you should begin to sell its shares. The fund could be turning over a large part of its portfolio, switching emphasis from weaker to stronger industry groups, and recovering before long. As it was dropping, so was your average cost, if you were still buying shares by dollar-cost averaging.

If you're in a fund with weekly betas exceeding 1.25 during an advancing market, you may be maximizing your gains—especially if the fund appears to be picking up momentum. If you're continuing to invest in it at increasingly higher prices, you are, of course, incurring greater risk. You should be able to relax, however, if that risk is offset by your holdings of one or more lower-beta funds. For it's your funds' combined volatility—your portfolio's beta—that sets your risk level.

Ideally, you want to be in funds whose betas are always greater than 1.0 when the market is rising, and less than 1.0 when it's falling. After all, that's the long-run goal for your portfolio.

If only it were unfailingly possible to identify such funds!

Given that this is not possible, you try to build and manage your portfolio in a way that enables you to profit from the stock market's unpredictable volatility. Since funds afford you the opportunity to increase or decrease portfolio volatility in small increments, they are useful vehicles for investment strategies. If you use low- or no-load funds, transactions cost little or nothing.

As your monitoring will reveal, the capability of superior funds to excel is not constant. An excellent fund may lag its own standard for a while, but the changes may be too small to matter if you are content with the indicated long-term return, and you are confident the slippage is temporary.

Explanations for temporary slippage are not hard to find. The strategies that managers and their shareholders find rewarding depend on the markets they operate in, and equity markets are continuously changing. Some managers do better in up markets, while others do better in down markets, but that's not the entire story.

Some, for example, do well with investments in small companies, and their betas should reflect their skills when stocks of small companies are in demand. They may not do as well in strong markets when stocks of large companies are more eagerly sought. This was amply demonstrated in 1986, when Lipper's average for small company growth funds had a return of only 5.64%—lowest of any Lipper group and less than half the all-funds median return of 13.99%.

If you remain confident in your fund portfolio manager's ability, don't want to take additional risks, and can afford to be patient, stay with the fund. Sooner or later, the market's leadership will change again and your manager's "kind of group" probably will regain its popularity.

What you want to be alert to is the probability that a "temporary" aberration becomes a clue to permanent deterioration in the portfolio manager's skills or to a decline in the attractiveness of your fund's group that may extend beyond your time horizon.

Quarterly Monitoring

Even the busiest investor should assess his portfolio at least once every three months. It's the most common frequency for the dissemination of data, by funds themselves and by reporting services, which enable you to analyze your portfolio and consider possible changes. It's also about as long as you'd want to ignore a fund before learning it's moving in the wrong direction.

Every three months, pick up the quarterly mutual funds issue of *Barron's* and determine in detail how your funds are doing.

Look for the *Barron's*/Lipper feature, "Top Funds Over Time," the tables of top and bottom funds for various periods (Figure 4-1), to see whether your funds are among the top 25 for the most recent 5 or 10 years. If one has dropped out, begin to redeem your shares by dollar-cost averaging out, putting the money into a money market fund until you find a new equity fund. If your funds remain listed, check "Top 100" (Figure 4-3) to see whether they also remain among the leading trough-to-peak performers. If any is not listed, begin to redeem your shares; you're not being adequately rewarded for taking risks.

When you turn to the *"Barron's*/Lipper Gauge" (see Figure 6-1), you will see each fund's performance expressed in terms of how an initial investment of $10,000 would have grown, or fallen, during a particular period if you had reinvested all dividends and capital gains distributions in shares of the same fund. (We recommend that you

FUND NAME	OBJ.	LOAD	TOTAL NET ASTS (MIL) 6/30/87	NAV 6/30/87	PERFORMANCE (RETURN ON INITIAL $10,000 INVESTMENT) 12/31/86- 6/30/87	6/30/86- 6/30/87	6/30/85- 6/30/87	6/30/82- 6/30/87	YIELD % 6/30/87	PER SHARE LATEST 12 MONTHS CAP GAINS	INC DIVS	LATEST AVAILABLE PRICE/ EARNINGS	ANNUAL % TURNOVER
ABT EMERGING GROWTH	CA	SC	49.0	10.67	12,166.50	$10,389.50	*	$	0.0	$ 0.00	$ 0.00	29.3	49
ABT GROWTH INCOME TR	GI	SC	139.9	14.05	12,516.60	12,787.70	28,291.90	*	2.7	2.70	0.42	23.3	95
ABT SECURITY INCOME	GI	SC	16.9	11.74	11,231.20	11,480.60	*	*	1.2	0.82	0.15	N/A	200
ABT UTILITY INCOME FD	UT	SC	133.4	14.52	10,095.10	10,487.20	19,876.20	*	6.5	0.27	0.95	10.8	45
ACORN FUND (R)	SG	NO	525.8	44.04	11,053.40	11,462.60	30,728.60	*	0.5	4.44	0.25	25.8	34
ADAM INVESTORS	CA	LO	11.2	13.55	11,371.60	10,977.10	*	*	5.5	1.55	0.94	N/A	153
ADDISON CAPITAL	CA	LO	40.2	26.1	12,371.60	*	*	*	0.0	0.00	0.00	N/A	N/A
ADTEK FUND	CA	NO	21.2	12.18	12,125.00	11,887.20	*	*	1.5	1.56	0.20	N/A	232
ADVANTAGE TRUS GOVT	FI	NO	257.4	9.80	9,951.30	*	*	*	0.0	0.24	0.15	N/A	N/A
ADVEST ADVANTAGE GOVT (R)	FI	NO	29.9	9.29	9,720.90	10,224.70	*	*	7.1	0.33	0.66	N/A	282
ADVEST ADVANTAGE GRO (R)	G	NO	67.2	12.90	12,252.90	12,015.50	*	*	0.3	0.45	0.03	N/A	33
ADVEST ADVANTAGE INC (R)	_	NO	4.6	10.55	10,587.90	11,117.30	*	*	4.1	0.00	0.68	N/A	79
ADVEST ADVANTAGE SPEC (R)	CA	NO	241.0	9.85	9,733.20	*	*	*	0.0	0.00	0.00	N/A	28
AETNA INCOME SHARES	FI	NO	4,004.2	13.14	10,023.80	10,610.40	21,386.60	*	7.3	0.00	1.01	12.3	31
AFFILIATED FUND	GI	LO	13.8	12.58	12,243.70	12,535.00	33,713.60	*	4.0	1.14	0.53	28.4	54
AFUTURE FUND	G	NO	2.4	3.59	11,374.00	9,008.30	14,223.10	*	0.0	2.18	0.00	N/A	22
AGE HIGH INCOME (R)	FI	LO	5.8	9.39	10,348.70	10,599.50	22,267.40	*	12.7	0.00	0.45	N/A	200
ALGER FIXED INCOME (R)	FI	NO	4.1	11.77	9,645.30	*	*	*	0.0	0.00	0.47	N/A	N/A
ALGER GROWTH (R)	G	NO	2.3	9.55	12,109.10	*	*	*	0.0	0.00	0.00	N/A	N/A
ALGER HIGH YIELD (R)	FI	NO	3.9	10.96	10,355.00	*	*	*	0.0	0.00	0.64	N/A	N/A
ALGER INCOME & GROWTH (R)	GI	NO	120.2	12.29	11,140.90	*	*	*	0.0	0.00	0.00	N/A	N/A
ALGER SMALL CAPITAL (R)	SG	NO	467.4	14.13	12,657.10	*	*	*	0.6	0.11	0.09	N/A	5
ALLEGRO GROWTH	G	NO	495.6	9.47	12,152.40	12,567.40	*	*	4.5	0.55	0.73	14.9	27
ALLIANCE BALANCED FUND	B	SC	27.3	8.90	11,071.20	10,371.20	30,051.60	*	12.8	0.00	1.21	N/A	109
ALLIANCE BOND-HIGH YLD	FI	FI	122.1	8.59	10,376.00	10,699.20	*	*	10.9	0.00	0.76	N/A	193
ALLIANCE BOND-US GOVT	FI	FI	53.0	10.26	10,126.60	12,227.40	25,950.40	*	1.3	1.20	0.53	28.3	94
ALLIANCE CANADIAN FUND	IF	SC	404.1	17.19	12,665.00	10,936.60	*	*	3.2	0.00	0.53	56	56
ALLIANCE CONVERTIBLE	CV	SC	948.2	4.13	11,993.20	11,757.40	*	*	3.5	0.00	0.34	16.5	17
ALLIANCE COUNTERPOINT	GI	SC	11.8	8.64	12,282.40	11,653.10	32,267.20	*	2.9	0.48	0.31	19.1	11
ALLIANCE DIVIDEND SHARES	GI	SC	194.7	11.48	11,653.10	11,742.70	26,397.20	*	2.9	2.07	0.04	26.5	44
ALLIANCE FUND	GI	SC	4.3	23.70	11,742.70	11,401.10	*	*	1.1	2.75	0.00	26.5	126
ALLIANCE GLOBAL	GL	SC	75.9	12.24	11,401.10	12,305.40	38,507.90	*	0.3	0.00	0.03	N/A	62
ALLIANCE INTERNATIONAL	IF	SC	200.8	9.29	12,305.40	10,757.00	23,395.70	*	9.1	2.75	0.00	N/A	240
ALLIANCE MONTHLY INCOME	FI	SC	32.8	31.86	10,122.30	10,082.60	*	*	10.9	0.02	1.01	N/A	190
ALLIANCE MORTGAGE INC	FI	SC	99.9	8.76	10,082.60	13,849.90	41,540.80	*	0.7	1.60	0.06	N/A	141
ALLIANCE TECHNOLOGY	TK	SC	13.7	25.94	14,625.90	11,549.60	31,710.00	*	0.7	0.90	0.36	56.7	35
ALPHA FUND	G	SC	2,959.9	15.26	12,800.30	11,440.40	*	*	0.8	0.00	1.22	22.9	63
AARP CAPITAL GROWTH	G	NO	320.2	15.48	12,241.60	11,923.00	*	*	0.3	0.23	0.01	N/A	62
AARP GENERAL BOND	FI	NO	3.3	24.44	9,921.00	11,414.80	*	*	8.8	0.08	1.36	N/A	37
AARP GNMA	FI	NO	1,093.7	11.46	11,414.80	11,727.30	*	*	2.4	0.50	0.64	N/A	N/A
AARP GROWTH AND INCOME	EI	NO	1,146.7	11.92	11,727.30	12,873.20	27,786.80	*	1.5	0.97	0.27	27.1	17
AMANA MUTUAL-INCOME	B	NO	231.3	17.74	12,628.00	12,540.30	23,138.40	*	2.0	0.98	0.18	28.1	59
AMCAP FUND	G	SC	719.2	7.16	11,374.10	12,645.30	29,113.70	*	2.8	1.73	0.64	24.6	48
AMERICAN BALANCED FUND	CA	SC	86.4	15.22	12,779.60	10,651.50	22,633.50	*	13.3	0.00	0.37	30	30
AMER CAPITAL COMSTOCK	FI	SC	8,847.1	13.17	10,380.10	11,399.70	26,909.50	*	1.3	1.02	0.81	24.8	90
AMER CAPITAL CORP BOND	FI	SC	34.2	10.84	11,399.70	10,254.40	*	*	7.3	0.44	0.93	N/A	N/A
AMER CAPITAL ENTERPRISE	CV	NO	437.5	27.18	9,753.20	10,324.50	23,221.70	*	7.3	0.59	0.05	29.3	411
AMER CAPITAL FED MORT	FI	SC	595.9	14.77	10,324.50	11,342.30	27,628.40	*	0.1	3.79	0.83	17.2	139
AMER CAPITAL GOVT	G	SC	36.7	9.86	13,530.40	10,942.00	22,506.70	*	5.5	1.06	0.08	N/A	83
AMER CAPITAL GROWTH	FI	SC	128.8	11.39	11,426.70	10,377.60	*	*	13.1	1.29	1.29	33.0	86
AMER CAPITAL HARBOR	SG	SC	12.8	9.12	10,700.70	11,455.90	*	*	0.9	0.33	0.00	N/A	268
AMER CAPITAL HIGH YIELD	CA	SC	3,000.5	10.20	12,315.40	10,014.90	30,304.68	*	8.3	0.90	0.82	33.8	115
AMER CAPITAL LIFE STOCK	CA	SC	353.3	28.94	9,770.20	12,653.40	22,069.30	*	1.2	0.83	0.01	33.0	107
AMER CAPITAL LIFE GOVT	G	SC	72.5	18.14	12,289.20	10,849.40	22,675.80	*	2.2	0.29	0.65	24.0	33
AMER CAPITAL PACE	CA	NO	0.7	9.28	12,822.30	11,520.60	8,415.30	*	1.2	1.09	0.29	30.9	105
AMER CAPITAL VENTURE	CA	SC		1.65	12,467.40	9,954.10	*	*	3.2	0.34	0.29	24.2	166
AMERICAN GROWTH	G	SC			12,293.00				0.0	0.00	0.00		N/A
AMERICAN HERITAGE	CA	NO			11,619.70								

Figure 6-1. A Sampling of Quarterly Mutual Fund Data. Source: Lipper Analytical Services, Inc., as it appeared in Barron's August 10, 1987. Excerpt from Barron's/Lipper Gauge shows types of data published quarterly for more than 1,200 funds.

reinvest. It doesn't only simplify your calculations; if you're in the right funds, it also should make you rich faster.)

While, of course, you could readily compare the *dollar* amounts for various funds with one another, you really should know your funds' performance in terms of their annualized *rates of return*. This knowledge is essential for at least four reasons:

1. It enables you to compare your funds with the S&P 500's performance (adjusted to reflect reinvestment of dividends) so that you have a better perspective than your weekly readings provide. For a down quarter, a drop which exceeds that of the S&P 500 by 5% is a major cause for concern.

2. You'll be able to compare each fund's performance for the latest year with that of its group's average, found in the table, "Mutual Fund Averages by Group" (Figure 6-2).

3. By reviewing similar quarterly performance data for your funds and the S&P 500 for, say, 2 years, you get an even longer-range perspective. You can see whether your funds are gaining or losing momentum or simply keeping pace with the market. It's possible, for example, to discover that a fund with a compounded annual rate of 20% for 5 years may have achieved it with very sharp gains in the first 3 years, and have slipped to a 10% rate in the last couple of years.

4. By comparing the growth (decline) rates for your funds with the long-term growth rates which you had originally established for your portfolio, you know whether your mutual fund strategy is on target. (You also may be less impressed by ads for other funds. See box on page 170.)

The percentage by which the theoretical $10,000 investment in each of your funds rose or fell during the most recent quarter or year to date can be readily annualized with a hand calculator. Converting the growth or decline of a $10,000 investment during the latest year

Mutual Fund Averages by Group

No. of Current Funds	Type of Fund	Total Reinvested Cumulative Performance 6/30/77- 6/30/87	6/30/82- 6/30/87	6/30/86- 6/30/87	12/31/86- 6/30/87	3/31/87- 6/30/87
147	Capital Appreciation Funds	+ 510.67%	+ 175.49%	+ 15.26%	+ 24.25%	+ 1.70%
230	Growth Funds	+ 436.34%	+ 177.96%	+ 14.48%	+ 22.33%	+ 1.78%
51	Small Company Growth Funds	+ 460.80%	+ 158.95%	+ 5.91%	+ 21.57%	− 0.68%
151	Growth and Income Funds	+ 361.32%	+ 191.98%	+ 16.87%	+ 19.08%	+ 2.57%
43	Equity Income Funds	+ 370.55%	+ 176.68%	+ 11.10%	+ 10.38%	+ 0.05%
622	General Equity Funds Average	+ 424.26%	+ 180.18%	+ 14.32%	+ 21.09%	+ 1.63%
7	Health Funds	+ 0.00%	+ 202.74%	+ 11.56%	+ 27.53%	+ 0.68%
11	Natural Resources Funds	+ 256.93%	+ 118.39%	+ 42.94%	+ 32.93%	+ 5.79%
25	Science & Technol. Funds	+ 402.97%	+ 164.41%	+ 21.19%	+ 28.02%	+ 1.44%
9	Utility Funds	+ 235.28%	+ 161.75%	+ 2.88%	+ 0.35%	− 3.10%
41	Specialty Funds	+ 332.04%	+ 230.20%	+ 10.50%	+ 19.53%	− 0.19%
32	Global Funds	+ 586.89%	+ 255.15%	+ 26.75%	+ 22.39%	+ 4.89%
48	International Funds	+ 495.84%	+ 297.37%	+ 41.48%	+ 25.75%	+ 7.79%
24	Gold Oriented Funds	+ 758.97%	+ 173.50%	+ 95.52%	+ 46.14%	− 2.10%
4	Option Growth Funds	+ 244.89%	+ 132.36%	+ 13.91%	+ 17.69%	+ 3.31%
19	Option Income Funds	+ 238.12%	+ 112.70%	+ 15.32%	+ 15.12%	+ 3.55%
842	All Equity Funds Average	+ 428.02%	+ 182.39%	+ 18.98%	+ 22.12%	+ 1.93%
22	Conv. Secs Funds	+ 360.23%	+ 158.71%	+ 7.17%	+ 10.28%	− 0.13%
37	Balanced Funds	+ 304.14%	+ 185.94%	+ 13.51%	+ 12.39%	+ 0.92%
21	Income Funds	+ 242.57%	+ 128.16%	+ 6.63%	+ 4.35%	− 1.45%
9	World Income Funds	+ 0.00%	+ 147.51%	+ 18.19%	+ 8.36%	− 0.60%
347	Fixed Income Funds	+ 153.29%	+ 114.00%	+ 5.51%	+ 0.70%	− 1.92%
1278	All Funds Average	+ 375.60%	+ 168.02%	+ 14.95%	+ 15.52%	+ 0.76%
1278	All Funds-Median	+ 339.98%	+ 167.22%	+ 11.21%	+ 16.49%	+ 0.71%
	No. of Funds in Universe With a % Change	394	516	1055	1179	1247

Value 6/30/87		Unmanaged Indexes Without Dividends Cumulative Performance				
2418.53	Dow Jones Ind Average	+ 163.95%	+ 197.87%	+ 27.78%	+ 27.56%	+ 4.94%
304.00	Standard & Poor's 500	+ 202.55%	+ 177.35%	+ 21.19%	+ 25.53%	+ 4.22%
352.98	Standard & Poor's 400	+ 218.80%	+ 188.34%	+ 26.16%	+ 30.77%	+ 5.20%
171.07	NYSE Composite	+ 210.47%	+ 171.45%	+ 18.83%	+ 23.45%	+ 3.12%
338.13	ASE Index	+ 462.05%	+ 169.65%	+ 18.98%	+ 28.44%	+ 1.64%

		Estimated Reinvested Unmanaged Indexes Cumulative Performance				
*2418.52	Dow Jones Ind Reinvested	+ 347.34%	+ 273.19%	+ 32.17%	+ 29.56%	+ 5.76%
*304.00	S&P 500 Reinvested	+ 388.28%	+ 242.46%	+ 25.17%	+ 27.44%	+ 5.02%

5/31/87		5/31/77- 5/31/87	5/31/82- 5/31/87	5/31/86- 5/31/87	11/30/86- 5/31/87	2/28/87- 5/31/87
338.70	Consumer Price Index	+ 87.54%	+ 17.97%	+ 3.80%	+ 2.39%	+ 1.29%

The method of calculating total return data on indexes utilizes actual dividends on x-dates accumulated for the quarter and reinvested at quarter end. This calculation is at variance with SEC release 327 of Aug. 6, 1972, which utilizes latest 12-month dividends. The latter method is the one used by Standard & Poor's.

Source: Lipper Analytical Services Inc.

Figure 6-2. Quarterly Scorecard for Fund Groups. Source: Lipper Analytical Services, Inc., as it appeared in *Barron's* August 10, 1987. (Group data for other periods are published weekly.)

to a percentage figure, naturally, requires no annualizing. But you will need the calculator to obtain the annual rate of return for every fund for the 5-year period ended with the latest quarter.

As you compare the annual rates of return for 3-month, year to

RETURN RATE GIMMICKS

If you calculate that your portfolio is growing at an annual rate of, say, 20%, and you read that professional money managers are tickled to earn a return at that level over time, what are you to think when you see mutual fund ads boasting of returns of 1,000% or more? It depends.

Before wondering about your ability to manage your own money, read the fine print in the ad. See what period it refers to: from when to when. Often the period begins with the formation of the particular fund and ends with the most recent month or calendar quarter. Since these are not the periods for which reporting services are likely to have kept and disseminated data, it'll be a bit difficult to derive the annual rate at which an investment in the fund would have been compounding. An easier comparison for you—if your calculator handles compound rates—will be with data for whole years. This can be revealing.

Take, for example, the returns of the Magellan Fund for the 15, 10, and 5 years ended 1986—periods in which it led all other funds covered by Lipper:

Period	Total Return for Period	Annual Rate
15 years	1,721.83%	21.35%
10 years	1,577.50	32.58
5 years	270.75	29.96

Impressive annual rates? Sure. But as dazzling as the total returns imply? Probably not.

Let's try another comparison using the funds which came in 25th in the Lipper rankings for each period: American Mutual, New York Venture, and United Continental Income, respectively:

Period	Total Return for Period	Annual Rate
15 years	656.10%	14.44%
10 years	584.81	21.22
5 years	196.44	24.28

With these data in mind, perhaps you'll look at the next ad more calmly—if you bother to look at all.

date, 1-year, and 5-year periods for your funds with one another and with the S&P 500, you will note that rates for longer periods often—but not always—tend to be lower than those for short ones. Since rates for short periods tend to be more volatile, it's those for the longer periods that you should use to assess and project your portfolio's performance.

MANAGERIAL CHANGES

Because of the high correlation between a fund's performance and its portfolio manager's strategy and skill, you should watch for any announcements of changes. This is more easily said than done because, unfortunately, such announcements can be made anywhere, at any time, or they may not be made at all.

Since funds are not required to disclose the identity of their portfolio managers in prospectuses or periodic reports to shareholders, announcements of managerial changes are not required either.

The law is quite clear on what shareholders are entitled to know about a fund's relationship with its investment adviser, but that is a company—often having the same ownership as the organization sponsoring the fund—not a person.

A portfolio manager, typically an employee, if not an officer of the investment adviser, may leave and be replaced without changing the validity of a fund's investment adviser contract. Thus no notice to shareholders is mandated.*

So what can you do? Keep your eyes open. Newspapers, especially *The Wall Street Journal,* and mutual fund newsletters occasionally carry news of managerial changes—perhaps a large share of those

---

*The portfolio manager, investment adviser, and fund management company are essentially synonymous in a number of cases. Albert O. Nicholas, for example, is president of Nicholas Fund, Inc., which contracted with Nicholas Company, Inc., for which he is portfolio manager, to be its investment adviser. It seems unlikely that Nicholas Fund would soon switch to a new portfolio manager; he's also president of Nicholas Company and its sole owner.

you'd be interested in. Alternatively, you can call each of your funds periodically and ask who the portfolio manager is.

If the name is a new one, your course of action is pretty clear: get out. Unless a new manager has been an understudy, and the board of directors (trustees) of the investment adviser or fund makes it clear that he or she can, and will, adhere to the fund's policies, or has made an impressive record at another fund, you really don't know what he or she can do for you. You might as well invest in another fund of which you know nothing, as bet on someone whose record is unknown—or who simply has no record.

We dwell on this point because managerial changes among mutual funds may occur as frequently as they do in other businesses—and because they have an even more important impact on your wealth.

When fund portfolio managers change, they do so for reasons common to business generally: They accept offers of more money or retire. They also may leave for a reason unique to mutual funds: A fund's performance has attracted so much new money from investors that the manager can no longer apply the same discipline (such as specializing in small companies) with the same attention-getting success as he or she could when the fund was smaller. Therefore, the manager would leave to run a new small fund and build a new record there.

You may have noted that we didn't raise the possibility that a managerial change could improve a fund's performance. That, of course, would occur with funds that have dismal records—not the sort that you would have invested in if you had used our screens. Figure 6-3, taken from Manhattan Fund's prospectus, shows what can happen when a change in investment adviser and portfolio manager occurs at a fund with a poor performance record.

ASSET ALLOCATION

When you invested in your funds, you presumably got an idea of how their assets were allocated from the prospectuses and latest periodic reports. And, as we've discussed, you probably have known generally

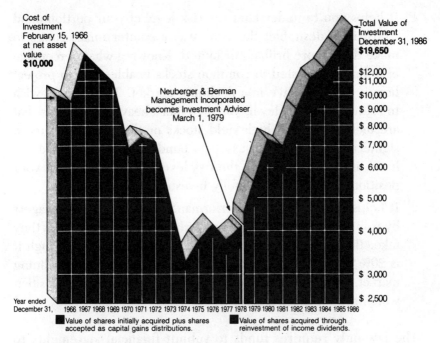

Cost of
Investment
February 15, 1966
at net asset
value
$10,000

Neuberger & Berman
Management Incorporated
becomes Investment Adviser
March 1, 1979

Total Value of
Investment
December 31, 1986
$19,650

$12,000
$11,000
$10,000
$ 9,000
$ 8,000
$ 7,000
$ 6,000
$ 5,000
$ 4,000
$ 3,000
$ 2,500

Year ended
December 31, 1966 1967 1968 1969 1970 1971 1972 1973 1974 1975 1976 1977 1978 1979 1980 1981 1982 1983 1984 1985 1986

■ Value of shares initially acquired plus shares
accepted as capital gains distributions.

■ Value of shares acquired through
reinvestment of income dividends.

Figure 6-3. The Difference an Investment Adviser Can Make. In its prospectus, Manhattan Fund does more each year than satisfy the legal requirement to disclose a change in investment advisers. It vividly depicts the change in the fund's fortunes since Neuberger & Berman took over in 1979, no doubt helped at least slightly by the remarkable bull market of the 1980s.

what kind of performance to expect of them. A fund that's 90% or more in common stocks and the rest in cash behaves differently from one that's 80% in stocks, and both have little in common with one that's 40% in stocks, 50% in bonds, and 10% in cash.

Some portfolio managers proclaim that they are, and will remain, 95% or more in stocks, but many adjust asset allocations as market conditions change—to become more aggressive or more defensive. You'll want to know what, if any changes, your managers have made in allocations. This information is useful primarily for two reasons:

1. It helps you to understand the risk level of your portfolio and adjust it, if desirable, the same way a painter mixes colors to make them more brilliant or muted. Knowing what percentage of a fund is invested in common stocks enables you to project how it might behave in a declining market. Thus, if you wish to reduce your risk level, you'd go more heavily into funds that are inclined toward high-yield stocks or that have allocated a significant share of their assets to bonds or cash. On the other hand, if you wish to raise the risk level, you'd strengthen your position in funds that are fully invested in stocks.

2. It helps you to assess the performance of your funds' managers by comparing their total returns with the extent of the risks they take. If a fund is keeping up with the S&P 500 even though it is 20% or more in cash, that's a very good sign. In a declining market, your interest will be protected by the defensive position which the manager has taken.

The law only requires funds to submit financial statements to shareholders semiannually, but the more enlightened fund managements provide them quarterly. If you own shares in a fund which is not one of these, you'll just have to find out what you can by phone. It should be enough to learn what percent of assets is in common stocks and what percent in cash. You don't need to bother with other asset categories, unless a fund is heavily in fixed-income securities and you want to see whether, and how, their portions of the total are changing.

FUND SIZE

The assets of mutual funds grow in essentially two ways: an increase in the value of their investments and a net inflow of money for the purchase of shares over the outflow to satisfy redemptions.

The two reinforce each other. When a funds' stock selections include some big winners and the aggregate market value of assets rises, new money comes pouring in and redemptions remain relatively low. The opposite is also true. Let a fund's investments slump, and a flood of requests for redemptions ensues, possibly causing a fund to liquidate holdings at depressed prices if not enough cash is available.

In a bull market such as that which began in 1982, the former was the more prevalent case. Many funds grew rapidly and shareholders experienced mixed results. Some were able to put new money to work effectively, as quickly as it came in, without affecting their performance in an environment of rising stock prices. Some were not.

Some of the better performers, unwilling to risk slippage in their returns by accepting purchases when there were no "bargains" for them to invest in, closed the funds to new investors. (See the following.)

In theory, a large equity fund should not be able to do as well as a small one, but in practice some do very well. Thus, having watched the exceptions to the rule, we feel some ambivalence about advocating strict rules regarding size and their rigid adherence.

We wouldn't suggest that you sell out of a fund as soon as its assets exceed a certain level. But we do suggest that you seriously consider liquidating your position if you're in an aggressive growth or growth fund that reaches a certain size AND conveys the impression of slipping performance. (It's not necessary to get out of a defensive fund such as Mutual Shares—one that has a beta of .40 to .50—even though it's large: being invested in many stocks reduces its volatility.)

Specifically, we recommend you consider getting out of a fund when its assets exceed $750 million if:

1. Its total return for the last 2 years has not exceeded that of the S&P 500, and

2. If you see no indication of better-than-market performance in declining markets.

If you have found another prospect that meets the criteria in the selection screens, you should not hesitate to move.

CLOSING OF FUNDS

Once in a while, mutual funds do what few other businesses do: turn down cash.

When a fund's performance attracts more cash from current and new investors than its portfolio manager believes he or she can invest profitably, it may suspend sales of shares to everyone or only to new investors.

If it were to continue to take all the cash that's offered, and could not find stocks at attractive prices, it would have to invest in Treasury bills or other short-term securities or less attractive investments, thereby depressing its rate of return.

The pattern among funds has been mixed. Vanguard's Windsor Fund did not suspend sales until it reached $3.4 billion in assets, while others did so while they were still much smaller (Table 6-3). Some have resumed sales of shares to all investors (Table 6-4), but at this writing a number have not. Some have suspended and resumed sales more than once.

Suspension of sales does not guarantee superior performance, even though Table 6-3 does include fine performers, any more than continuous sales of new shares guarantees inferior performance. If you're in a fund when it suspends sales, you're probably better off staying with it. If you're considering a fund after it has resumed share sales, we'd go along if, of course, the fund passes the screens.

CHANGE IN OBJECTIVES

Under the Investment Company Act, a newly organized mutual fund has a great deal of discretion with respect to the investment policy and practices it may pursue. To register its securities with the SEC, a fund simply has to state its investment policy and proposed tactics in the registration statement.

Once committed, the fund can only change fundamental objectives with the consent of shareholders. This means that, as a shareholder,

TABLE 6-3. Some Funds That Closed to New Investors . . .

Fund	Year of Sales Suspension	Assets Size at Closing (in Millions)
Lindner	1984	$ 339
Lindner Dividend	1985	68
Loomis-Sayles Capital Development	1969	58
Penn Mutual	1984	300
Quasar	1986	167
Sequoia	1982	247
Vanguard Explorer	1985	360
Vanguard Qualified Dividend I	1985	112
Vanguard Windsor	1985	3,400

TABLE 6-4. . . . And Some That Have Reopened

Fund	Year of Sales Suspension	Assets Size at Closing (in Millions)	Year of Sales Resumption	Assets Size at Resumption (in Millions)
Fidelity Magellan	1965	$ 4	1981	$ 90
Mutual Qualified Income	1986	480	1986	500
Mutual Qualified Income	1987	731	1987	760
Mutual Shares	1986	1,200	1986	1,300
Mutual Shares	1987	1,800	1987	1,900
Nicholas II	1986	261	1986	301
Price (T.R.) New Horizons	1967	105	1970	138
Price (T.R.) New Horizons	1972	464	1974	191
Royce Value	1985	84	1986	115

you will receive a proxy notice when the management of one of your funds wants to change policy. You'll also get a proxy card entitling you to vote.

You will want to think seriously about any proposal. It's not that your vote might make the difference between a proposal's passing or losing. Rather, it's that a proposal might change the nature of a fund enough that instead of, or in addition to, using the proxy card you decide to withdraw from the fund.

Perhaps the most common changes have to do with the industries in which a fund might concentrate its investments and the types of securities it might invest in besides stocks and bonds.

If such a change is likely to increase a fund's risk level higher than you'd like, or if it takes the fund in a direction you don't want to go, we suggest selling after the proxies are counted and you know the proposal carried. If the issue is an important one, and you're not sure that you fully understand it after reading management's statement, you may want to be on the lookout for comments in mutual fund newsletters or newspapers.

INCREASES IN COSTS

The three major types of mutual fund costs—front-end loads, 12b-1 distribution charges, and redemption fees—have to be disclosed in a prospectus, although the statements of disclosure are not always easy to find.

If a fund adopts a cost it has not had before, or if it raises the level of an existing charge, it must make this known in a supplement to the existing prospectus until a new one is printed. If you already own the shares, you must be notified. If you're considering the fund, you'll find out when you get the prospectus.

We believe everyone is entitled to fair pay for services rendered, but we also believe one does not need to invest in funds imposing any of these charges if one has the opportunity to invest in a pure no-load fund of equal merit. It could be that a fund's performance is

so good that such costs seem negligible in comparison, and performance is, after all, what matters most. But when the inevitable market
drops occur, excessive costs will simply encumber the fund's rate of
return.

Thus if you're notified that a charge is being levied to reimburse
the fund for distribution expenses, or to console it for your desire to
redeem your shares, we'd suggest leaving it during the time you'll
be given for doing so. It makes no sense to agree to have your return
shaved for services that don't benefit you directly.

We have no similar objection to fees charged by an investment
adviser to manage a fund's portfolio, which also have to be detailed
in the prospectus, so long as they are reasonable and the firm is doing
a good job of indirectly managing your money.

If your fund proposes an increase in this fee which would not have
a significant effect on your return, we'd stay with it—provided you're
satisfied with the fund's performance.

An entirely different cost increase occurs when a fund increases
the rate at which it turns over its portfolio and thereby exposes you
involuntarily to tax liabilities for undesired capital gains distributions.
There's nothing you can do about capital gains already taken; the fund
doesn't have to ask shareholders for permission to take capital gains.

But for the future you'll want to check the financial statement to
see whether a fund is lifting its turnover rate. Unless you hold the
fund shares in an IRA, you may want to switch to a fund with similar
attributes but a lower turnover rate.

7

A CYCLICAL STRATEGY TO ENHANCE YOUR RETURNS

For those of you who are individual or institutional investors (such as pension fund managers) with larger financial assets and longer horizons than most individual investors, we offer in this chapter some strategies for enhancing returns on mutual fund investments.

In contrast with the previous material in this book, which is aimed primarily at those with lower levels of assets and less time to devote to their management, this chapter addresses those of you whose horizons are typically longer, who can tolerate slightly

181

higher levels of volatility to produce increments in rates of return over the long term, and who can and will spend more time managing assets. It assumes you have some experience with investing in equity mutual funds—say, ownership of shares of three or more over a period of three or more years.

To put it simply, the objective of this chapter is to help you to achieve greater returns in two ways:

1. By reducing your investment in funds before they hit their cyclical peaks and drop in value. Investments that have run up are at higher risk—the higher they are, the riskier they are.

2. By investing the proceeds and/or fresh cash in funds which appear to be gaining momentum.

As you buy and sell, you'll always want to be certain that your portfolio remains suitably diversified among two or three of the broad fund groups—aggressive growth, growth, growth and income, equity income, balanced, and international/global—to control your exposure to risk. While the simplicity of the index fund (see box) approach has its understandable appeal to many, we think that you can do better with a little effort.

Because we believe that even an active wealthy investor need not be an aggressive one to achieve superior results, we urge the same tactics—easing in and easing out—that we have recommended for people of more modest means.

ROTATION OF MARKET LEADERSHIP

Although most aspects of investing in securities can be predicted with little confidence, you can assign a higher level of probability to the sequence in which leadership among economic sectors rotates as market averages fluctuate from peak to trough and back to peak again.

Peaks are typically characterized by strength—often excesses—in highly speculative stocks while market bottoms find the bluest of the

SHOULD YOU CONSIDER AN INDEX FUND?

You may be inclined to forego the time and trouble involved in selecting equity funds and simply want to invest in an index fund—one whose principal objective is to match the performance of an established common stock index, such as the S&P 500. "Since only one fund manager out of every four outperforms the S&P 500," you might say, "it is also true that an index fund will outperform three out of four fund managers."

The question would be easy to deal with if you could predict the future. If you thought you could not find the one fund in four that outperforms the average, an index fund might be a good idea. If, on the other hand, you believe that you can do better, you would have no need for index funds. If doing as well—or as poorly—as the market is good enough for you, your portfolio will experience the same volatility as the market: that of a beta of 1.00. You will, thus, not endeavor to raise or lower the beta of your portfolio as market conditions change by adjusting its composition. (If you were to raise and lower cash with changing conditions, you would be engaging in market timing—something even few professionals do well.)

In the very long run, as we saw in Chapter 1, the average return of the S&P 500—and thus of an index fund—will probably continue to exceed the inflation rate, but may not equal the performance of well-run funds. In the short run, the S&P 500—and an index fund invested to match it—may hit an air pocket now and then. And even if the S&P 500 is rising, reflecting the performance of the stocks of large capitalization companies, an index fund may not do as well as funds with a different orientation, such as emerging growth companies.

While index mutual funds, with their limitations, have their place in some individual investors' portfolios, their conception and development in the mid-1970s were more of a response to the needs of certain institutional investors following enactment of the Employee Retirement Income Security Act (ERISA).

Commenting in its 1976 annual report on the first filing of a registration statement by a mutual fund wishing to adopt an index approach, similar to that already being followed by banks and large companies, the SEC said:

> The development of the index fund concept was accelerated with the recent enactment of federal pension reform legislation which imposes certain obligations on persons acting in a fiduciary capacity with respect to retirement fund invest-

ments. Index funds are seen by some as a means by which fiduciaries may discharge these obligations in a prudent manner while achieving the investment performance of a diversified pool of common stocks.

Ironically, the year of ERISA's enactment, 1974, saw the stock market taking an enormous drop—for the second consecutive year—which might have made some wonder whether equities were suitable investments for retirement fund assets.

By the time the Vanguard Index Trust was established on December 31, 1975 as the first index fund, the market had made a sensational recovery. The S&P 500 had gone up 31% that year (excluding dividends and their reinvestment)—a feat unmatched for a full year since, and one that would have made anyone happy to own shares of an index fund, if only one had been in existence.

On the other hand, at this writing in Summer 1987, five years after the bull market of the 1980s began, the S&P 500 was selling at more than 20 times earnings—a ratio that, by historical standards, indicated overvaluation. Depending on one's investment horizon, we would not hesitate to invest in equities, on a dollar-cost averaging basis, even at such times. But we would refrain from jumping on the index fund bandwagon, preferring to look for fund groups whose valuation seemed less generous.

blue chips in greatest demand, usually only by the relatively few who have the nerve—and the good sense—to buy stocks of any kind when all seems hopeless.

Between peaks and troughs, market leadership normally is passed along like a baton in a relay race. At the bottom, it is usually held by funds invested in companies in which people seek refuge when things look gloomiest: large companies paying good dividends (commonly held by equity income and growth and income funds). After a recovery is under way for a while and these companies are no longer the great bargains they were, market leadership is assumed by funds that are invested in companies that are not as huge and pay lower dividends (growth funds). These eventually yield leadership to funds holding shares in small but rapidly expanding companies that may not yet pay dividends at all (small company growth and capital appreciation funds).

Size of the companies in funds' portfolios is not the only factor which determines the relative strength of fund groups during the various stages of the market cycle. Rates of inflation, reflecting the stages of the business cycle, have their impact, too—whether on funds invested in stocks of interest-sensitive companies (e.g., banks, utilities) or on those in gold-mining and other natural resources companies, not to mention funds invested in bonds.

When interest rates seem about to rise with consumer prices as the economy becomes heated and investors seek to hedge their portfolios against inflation, interest-sensitive funds (balanced and income) give way to gold funds. When inflation has been arrested and interest rates are expected to fall, funds invested in interest-sensitive securities are favored again.

Viewed in the context of risk levels, the funds that are most desirable in an advancing market are those with the highest betas; in a declining market, those with the lowest betas (Table 7-1).

What you can try to do is raise the weighted average beta of your portfolio during an expansion and lower it during a market decline.

TABLE 7-1. Fund Groups Ranked By Levels of Risk

Fund Investment Objective	Beta
Aggressive Growth	1.12
Growth	.91
Growth & Income	.82
Balanced	.56
Bond	.18
S&P 500	1.00

Source: *"The Individual Investor's Guide to No-Load Mutual Funds"* (sixth edition), American Association of Individual Investors, Chicago.

Note: Although betas were calculated for international and precious metals funds, .58 and (.02), respectively, these groups' special characteristics limit the usefulness of their betas in building and adjusting portfolios.

As you make changes, make them gradually. Remember, you're dealing in probabilities—not certainties—and you don't want to exacerbate
risk by making shifts that suddenly and totally change your investment
posture. Happily, when you're dealing with mutual funds, gradual
changes are easy to implement.

REDUCING YOUR EXPOSURE

Since the avoidance of loss should always have the highest priority—
no matter how large or small your portfolio—your attention should
first be directed toward reducing your exposure if you own funds that
may be subjected to selling.

While your general knowledge of the market and your awareness
of what's going on will enable you to assess your portfolio and decide
whether one or more of your funds may be vulnerable, you don't
need to act only on your own subjective analysis. You can find help
in the Lipper statistics carried in the quarterly mutual funds issue of
Barron's.

When it comes out, we suggest you turn to the table, "Mutual
Fund Averages by Group" (Figure 6-2), which contains performance
data for groups of mutual funds for five periods, ranging from the last
10 or 15 years to the latest 3 months, as calculated by Lipper.

Focus on the column for the 5 years ended in the last quarter and
find the group which is up the most. Compare its percentage to the
one below for the S&P 500—the one which reflects reinvestment of
dividends. If the group's total return has increased 20% more than
that of the S&P 500, you could conclude that the group is close to
its cyclical peak—or at least that it's closer than other groups are to
their peaks.

If you own a fund in the group, it might be smart to begin easing
out of your position. (To see how Lipper classifies the funds you own,
turn to the *Barron's*/Lipper Gauge listing in the same issue.) If the
group led the S&P 500 by 30% or more, you might wish to accelerate
your redemptions. Should the group, in fact, go down, your timing

will have been sound and you could continue to redeem shares gradually. If the group continues to rise, you will have participated in the
increase by retaining a portion of your shares, but may wish to continue
selling more shares on the grounds that they have become even more
overpriced—and thus risky—than when you sold the first batch.

Repeat the procedure to see if one or more additional fund groups
also have exceeded the S&P 500's growth rate by 20% or more. Should
you own funds belonging to those groups, it might be prudent to
reduce your positions in those as well.

There may be extenuating circumstances to explain why a fund
group has outperformed all others and why it may be reasonable to
assume the group will continue to rise. But, generally speaking, wis-
dom would indicate selling a part of a position in securities that seem
overvalued by the market. Most of the time, the prudent course
probably will turn out to be the right course.

If you wish to confirm the desirability of selling shares of a fund
in a group that seems to be doing so well, we have a couple of suggestions:

1. Compare your fund's performance in the last quarter with that
   of the S&P 500, shown in the table. If your fund's total return
   for the quarter was less than one-half as much as the S&P 500
   (or if in a down quarter it had fallen more), that underperformance could indicate your fund is slowing down.
2. Look at the table, "Top 100" (Figure 4-3), to see whether your
   fund is listed for the period depicted. If not, or if it's listed but
   ranked at the bottom, you'd have another indication of slippage.

Don't be disappointed if you find no fund group as much as 20%
ahead of the S&P 500's 5-year growth rate, or if you don't have shares
in a fund that belonged to a group which was that much ahead. Such
findings could mean that the market has not yet reached excessive
levels, or that you have a fund whose manager's investment strategy
and stock selection skills have not yet been recognized.

While this technique of identifying possibly vulnerable funds may appear to be inconsistent with the screens suggested in Chapter 4, it is really only a refinement for those of you who wish to manage your portfolios more actively. It asks you to test your best-performing funds inferentially—in the absence of any direct test—for the likelihood that they will continue to profit in the next stage of the market cycle. Skilled as their managers may have been in the last stage, a change in the market environment could provide you with a choice of better prospects among funds that have been underperforming.

Although funds that have gone up a lot may continue to rise nicely for a while, there is a good chance that the performance of lagging fund types will begin to improve as a result of economic changes that benefit the companies whose shares they own. Switching cautiously to such funds could very well improve your returns.

ADDING TO YOUR POSITIONS

Whether you have proceeds from a sale which you wish to reinvest or fresh cash, you can use the same table, "Mutual Fund Averages by Group," in the same issue of *Barron's* for clues to help you to identify funds that are candidates for purchase.

Run down the same column for 5-year performance, but this time look for the broad fund group that has lagged the S&P 500 by the greatest margin for this period.

Then go to the table, "Performance Gauge" (Figure 4-1), and look at the top right for the list of the top 25 funds for the most recent quarter. If the lagging fund group is represented in the table by two or more funds, it might be an indication that the group is perking up and that it could be a timely purchase.

Submit the funds to the screens (Chapter 4) except those for 5- and 10-year performance. If one or both pass, begin to invest by dollar-cost averaging.

Should the next lowest group also be represented among the top 25, you could have additional candidates to be screened for purchase. Begin to invest in the funds that pass. And watch them.

If no group lagging the S&P 500 by 20% or more for 5 years is represented by two or more funds in the list, don't look for a new purchase candidate. Instead, if you have proceeds from a sale or new cash, add to the holdings of your present portfolio in a way that preserves its beta. If the market appears to be weakening, you may wish to reduce the beta. On the other hand, if market prospects are turning up, you could raise it.

EXAMPLES AND CONCLUDING COMMENTS

International and gold funds offer examples of how the method outlined in this chapter might have worked for you.

For the 5 years ended September 1985, according to Lipper, international funds were up 59% vs. 85% for the S&P 500. If you had glanced at the top 25 funds for the third quarter of 1985, you would have seen as many as 14 international funds. (Only one had been listed for the previous quarter.) Anyone acting on those clues would have enjoyed a spectacular return in 1986; the group as a whole, according to Lipper, was up 53% for the year—triple the S&P 500's total return.

Of course, growth of such proportions could have been regarded as too good to last. By the third quarter of 1986 Lipper's 5-year data showed the international group more than 20% ahead of the S&P 500, indicating an increase in the group's risk level—and a sign that investors should begin to withdraw slowly by dollar-cost averaging even as the group continued rising.

At the same time, gold funds, which had badly lagged the market—even shown *negative* total returns for 5-year periods—suddenly came to dominate the list of the third quarter's leaders, accounting for 20 of the top 25 places. Someone picking this up would have been rewarded soon: in only the first quarter of 1987, Lipper reported, gold funds were up 49%—more than double the market's rate.

This strategy is not without risks, and it may not always produce quick or equally gratifying results—recall the long time that gold funds underperformed. But it is a reasoned way of increasing participation in funds that do very well compared to the market and of decreasing participation in those that do less well. It is based on objective, well-regarded data that are easily accessible to anyone with a copy of *Barron's*, not on wishful thinking.

Over time investors following this approach should be rewarded by being in fund types that are emerging from periods of sluggishness and by not being in fund types that have become too risky. (Naturally, in initiating any purchases you'll want to bear in mind your own personal or institutional tolerance for risk.)

It is not impossible for anyone with time (or staff), money, and skills to develop and implement a similar strategy that uses individual securities, but the selection of mutual funds available today certainly make the job much simpler—and less costly.

Funds offer you unusually easy, even unique, opportunities to make choices between discrete types of investments while maintaining a requisite degree of diversification. They enable you to do this in a manner that raises or lowers portfolio volatility in increments as circumstances indicate.

By utilizing the classification system and performance data provided by Lipper, as suggested in this chapter, you should be able to identify fund types which would be appropriate to buy or sell—and to enhance your return by acting ahead of the crowd.

8

MUTUAL FUND TACTICS FOR IRAs

If having adequate retirement income is your major objective for building capital—or your only one—and if you haven't already done so, you owe it to yourself to establish one or more individual retirement accounts. And if you have an IRA, and have not already done so, you really ought to consider investing at least some of this money in mutual funds.

Perhaps you're surprised that we would still advocate IRAs following passage of the Tax Reform Act of 1986, which eliminated one of the benefits of an IRA for many people. Certainly the debate leading to its enactment and subsequent speculation about its consequences have confused many about the continuing desirability—and even the viability—of IRAs. Some people seem to have gotten the impression that IRAs were killed. Even *The New York Times* said in a headline on February 15, 1987: "An ambitious savings experiment comes to an end."

Happily, this is not the case. It is true that President Reagan, Representative Dan Rostenkowski, Senator Bob Packwood, and their fellow members of Congress deprived millions of Americans of the opportunity to take an income tax deduction for their annual contributions to IRAs, beginning in 1987—an incentive that the President and Congress had granted them just 5 years before. But, despite the politicians' flip-flop in the name of "tax simplification," "tax reform," or "revenue neutrality," IRAs are alive.

They are still helping millions to save for retirement during their working years by providing them an economically attractive and convenient way to accumulate capital without having to pay current income tax as the money is building up. This is why IRAs are sometimes facetiously referred to as "the tax shelter of the middle class."

During the 1986 debate, some called IRAs "a rich man's tax shelter" and tried to prove it with the help of statistics. It is apparently true, for example, that the net worth of a median family with an IRA is triple that of a family without one, or that a higher percentage of eligible high income taxpayers have IRAs than of lower income taxpayers. But it is also true that about 60% of tax returns reporting IRA contributions showed annual gross income of less than $40,000—hardly what you'd call rich.

We do not wish to take your time to replay the debate. Instead, we are interested—and we presume you are interested—in noting the advantages which an IRA may have for you, and in focusing on the role which mutual funds may have in your IRA strategy.

THE IRA CONCEPT

Proposed by President Nixon in a 1971 message on private pension reform, and incorporated in more limited form in the Employee Re-

tirement Income Security Act of 1974 (ERISA) that President Ford
signed shortly after he succeeded Nixon, IRAs were to serve one
principal purpose: to help employees to ensure that they would have
sufficient retirement income for themselves and their dependents.
Those who were not covered by an employer's pension plan and who
were otherwise eligible could put up to $1,500 per year into an IRA
and deduct the amount from their taxable income. Most, concerned
about the safety of the principal, deposited the money in commercial
banks, mutual savings banks, and savings and loan associations; many
bought certificates of deposit (CDs) bearing fixed rates of interest and
having terms up to five years or longer.

Instead of offering IRAs to all workers as a means of saving inde-
pendently to supplement other retirement income, such as Social Security and private pension benefits, as President Nixon had urged,
ERISA was endowed with a more limited objective: to help people
whose employers do not provide pensions, who switch employers
(voluntarily or involuntarily)) and thereby may suffer a reduction in
potential retirement benefits, or who are self-employed.

Partly to reflect concern for workers who change employers, ERISA
also created rollover IRAs in addition to, and separate from, the IRAs
to which employees made annual contributions. The Act permitted
everyone leaving an employer, as well as everyone retiring, to roll
over tax-free into these IRAs (1) a lump sum from an employer's tax-
qualified savings plan, (2) a lump sum offered in lieu of a lifetime of
monthly pension checks, or (3) both.

Seven years later, as the nation was entering a severe recession,
Congress had a change of heart. It passed and President Reagan signed
the Economic Recovery Act of 1981, containing not only sharp cuts
in individual income tax rates, but also a liberalization of the eligibility
requirements for IRAs, resembling those which Nixon had proposed.

Beginning in 1982, people who were covered by employers' pension
plans were also permitted to contribute to an IRA and to deduct the
amount from their taxable income. Moreover, Congress raised the
maximum contribution from earned—but not investment—income
from $1,500 per year to $2,000, plus $250 for a nonworking spouse.

Said the staff of the Joint Committee on Taxation:

The Congress was concerned that a large number of the country's workers, including many who are covered by employer-sponsored retirement plans, face the prospect of retiring without the resources needed to provide adequate retirement income levels. The Congress concluded that retirement savings by individuals during their working years can make an important contribution towards providing retirement income security.

Table 8-1 shows how quickly individuals responded. The number of individual income tax returns reporting contributions to IRAs soared from 3.4 million in 1981 to 12.0 million in 1982, and the amounts contributed rose even more sharply, from $4.8 billion to $28.3 billion. Both the number of returns showing contributions and the amounts continued to rise in ensuing years.

From $26.1 billion at the end of 1981, total IRA balances had grown to more than $250 billion by 1986, owing to the net of annual contributions and rollovers after distributions and to returns on participants' money. The total accounted for 2% of all households' financial assets.

Energizing this growth were the widespread desire to ensure adequate retirement income and three major features:

1. The ability to deduct annual IRA contributions (but not rollovers) from taxable income.

2. The ability to earn dividends, interest, and capital gains sheltered from current taxation, thereby having earnings compounding on a larger principal base.

3. The prospect of being in a lower tax bracket when the time comes to begin to take money out of IRAs and to pay taxes on it.

To be sure, a survey by the Investment Company Institute showed that the principal reason people gave for opening an IRA was to save on current taxes. But "supplement retirement income" and "Social Security inadequate" were not far behind. Two other reasons cited were "control financial future" and "good way to save."

TABLE 8-1. How Annual IRA Contributions Have Grown

	1975	1980	1981	1982	1983	1984	1985
Total Individual Income Tax Returns (in millions)	82.2	93.9	95.4	95.3	96.3	99.4	101.7
Returns with IRA Contributions (in millions)	1.2	2.6	3.4	12.0	13.6	15.2	16.4
Percent of Returns with IRA Contributions	1.5	2.7	3.6	12.6	14.1	15.3	16.1
Total Amount Contributed (in billions)	$1.4	$3.4	$4.8	$28.3	$32.1	$35.4	$38.7
Amount per Return	$1,185	$1,338	$1,391	$2,354	$2,355	2,322	$2,361

Source: *Statistics of Income Bulletin*, Internal Revenue Service

IRAs AFTER 1986 TAX REFORM

It is the deductibility of IRA contributions by people covered by pension plans and having earnings above certain income levels that the Tax Reform Act of 1986 took away. The tax code's IRA* provisions, most of them unchanged, now include:

1. Total deductibility of annual contributions, up to $2,000, for each employee and working spouse not covered by pension plans, regardless of income.

2. Total deductibility for those who *are* covered but whose gross adjusted income falls below certain levels.

3. Partial deductibility for those whose income is a bit higher but not too high.

4. The opportunity to contribute up to $250 for a "nonworking" spouse in certain circumstances.

5. The opportunity to contribute nondeductible money—that is, after-tax dollars—and the responsibility to keep proper records to distinguish nondeductible from deductible contributions.

6. The opportunity, at termination or retirement, to roll over money tax-free from an employer's qualified plan(s) into an IRA.

7. Deferral of any income tax liabilities on all interest, dividends, and capital gains earned in IRAs until money is taken out.

8. No money may be contributed after one is 70½ years of age.

9. Distribution *may* begin when one is 59½, but it *has to* begin by 70½.

10. When distribution begins, taxes are due at ordinary rates on all the money that's taken out. If one has made both deductible

*Before making any decision, be sure to check the actual rules. We've generalized because the precise regulations may be subject to change. Tax benefits available for retirement plans for the self-employed differ in some respects from IRAs.

and nondeductible contributions, distributions will be partly taxable and partly nontaxable.

11. If distribution from an IRA begins before one is 59½, a penalty has to be paid on the distribution in addition to the tax. (This was left at 10%.)

Within these parameters, opportunities to use IRAs need to be thought of in two ways:

1. If you're still earning income and retirement is years away, you may find it desirable to contribute to one or more IRAs, regardless of whether the money is deductible from your gross income.

If you're going to have the IRA for enough years, its tax-sheltered earnings could eventually provide you a considerably larger sum than if you invested the $2,000 annually outside of an IRA.

Rates of return and taxes may change, of course, but the Investment Company Institute supported this case with a calculation for the environment prevailing in early 1987. If you were in a 28% tax bracket and annually invested $2,000 to earn 9% outside an IRA, after 25 years you would have about $90,000. If you invested the same amount at the same yield in an IRA on a nondeductible basis, you'd have $133,000. Of course, if you were able to deduct the contributions, you'd have a lot more—about $185,000—before paying taxes on the amount you had deducted.

Who knows? Congress and a future administration may come up with a new tax reform package that undoes parts of the Tax Reform Act of 1986. As it was enacted, some members already were talking about restoring deductibility.

2. If you are going to retire soon (early or at the "normal" age of 65), or if you are going to be otherwise leaving an employer who has a savings plan or who offers you the choice of a lump sum in lieu of a monthly pension check, give serious consideration to a tax-free rollover into one or more IRAs.

IRA INVESTMENT CONSIDERATIONS

Having decided to consider an IRA for yourself, you have to think of what to do with the money. All that the Internal Revenue Code requires is that you "contribute" or "roll over" the money to an approved custodian or trustee who will keep it and invest it for you until the day you take the last cent out. Until you are 59½ you cannot spend it without paying an early withdrawal penalty, and you cannot borrow against it. A succession of Presidents and Congresses have wanted you to *save* the money for your retirement.

A custodian or trustee can be a commercial bank, mutual savings bank, savings and loan association, life insurance company, credit union, mutual fund, or stock brokerage firm which meets Internal Revenue Service qualifications. In the case of the latter, you can have what is known as a "self directed" account, comparable to an ordinary brokerage account, but with an IRA twist.

What you can ask these institutions to do with your IRA money also has to meet IRS requirements. They may buy shares of corporations' stocks or mutual funds, government or corporate bonds, certificates of deposit (CDs), annuities, or interests in limited partnerships, to name the principal investments. (Traditional lines have become blurred. Some banks now enable you to buy mutual fund shares, for example, while some mutual fund companies now offer stock purchase facilities.)

Table 8-2 shows how people have invested their IRA cash beginning with 1981, the year before IRA provisions were last liberalized.

Since it is likely that you will want to have some flexibility in anticipation of unforeseeable circumstances, it is important to bear in mind the rules on moving your money around. Regardless of whether yours is an annual contribution or rollover IRA, the government permits you to switch part or all of your money from one custodian or trustee to one or more others but limits how this must be done to two ways:

1. A "rollover" (different from the rollover from an employer's plan *into* an IRA) whereby you request a check from the first firm

TABLE 8-2. How IRA Assets Are Invested (In billions of dollars)

Institution	1981	1982	1983	1984	1985	1986
Commercial banks	$ 5.8	$13.6	$26.5	$ 37.2	$ 51.5	$ 67.0
Savings banks and savings and loans	14.1	20.3	31.7	43.4	56.4	69.0
Life Insurance Companies	3.3	5.8	9.0	12.6	16.9	22.0
Credit unions	.2	1.6	5.0	7.8	13.9	20.5
Mutual funds	2.6	5.7	10.7	16.5	31.6	53.7
Self directed accounts	NA	5.5	8.4	14.6	29.4	44.9
Total	$26.1	$52.4	$91.3	$132.1	$199.8	$277.1

NA = not available

Source: Investment Company Institute

and have 60 days in which to reinvest it with another. You can make such a move only once a year per account.

2. A "transfer" whereby you ask the first firm to send a check directly to one or more others, bypassing you altogether. The government imposes no limits on how often you can use a "trustee-to-trustee" transfer, but the trustees may have their own rules as well as fees. You may find that some, whether eager to manage your money a bit longer, overwhelmed, or just inefficient, are very slow to act on your request to transfer your money to somebody else.

USING MUTUAL FUNDS

Deciding where to open IRAs involves most of the same considerations that are involved in deciding what to do with money outside IRAs: your age, financial circumstances, objectives, tolerance for risk, and so forth. After analyzing your situation, you very well may find, as many others have, that mutual funds make a lot of sense for IRA investments.

Tables 8-3 and 8-4 show how mutual funds have been used by IRA investors in the 1980s. Clearly, as stock prices soared and interest rates fell, many have been increasingly inclined to take risks and leave a lower share of their IRA money in money market funds.

As accounts have become larger, more people probably have felt comfortable in incurring risks with at least a part of their IRA money. It's quite possible that an average annual contribution account will have grown to $15,000 or more. (Anyone who has contributed $2,000 annually beginning with 1982 will have put in $10,000 through 1986 and, presumably, will have enjoyed some income as well as capital appreciation in those years of rising securities prices.) The size of an average rollover account, however, is not known; the Investment Company Institute stopped keeping rollover data after 1980, and apparently no one else has begun.

TABLE 8-3. How Mutual Fund IRAs Are Invested (Including Money Market Funds) (Assets in billions)

Investment Objective	1981	1982	1983	1984	1985	1986
Aggressive Growth	$0.1	$0.6	$ 2.0	$ 2.7	$ 4.2	$ 6.2
Growth	.3	.6	2.0	2.8	4.3	6.3
Growth and Income	.2	.5	1.4	2.4	4.3	9.3
Precious metals	NA	NA	NA	NA	0.3	0.4
International	NA	NA	NA	NA	1.2	2.5
Balanced	*	*	*	0.1	0.2	0.7
Income	0.1	0.3	0.5	1.5	0.6	1.4
Option/income	*	0.1	0.1	0.3	0.8	0.7
Government Income	NA	NA	NA	NA	3.4	7.9
Ginnie Mae	NA	NA	NA	NA	2.2	4.0
Corporate Bond	0.3	0.7	1.3	1.9	3.6	5.8
Money Market	1.6	3.0	3.5	5.3	6.5	8.4
Total	$2.6	$5.8	$10.8	$16.9	$31.5	$53.7

* Less than $0.1 billion.
NA = not available.
Totals may not add due to rounding.
Source: Investment Company Institute.

If it makes sense for you to invest for growth of capital as well as income and, therefore, to allocate some of your IRA money to common stocks, we highly recommend mutual funds for the same reasons that we advocate them outside the context of IRAs and suggest you can adhere to the same criteria for fund selection.

As you consider the advantages which mutual funds offer IRAs, you might keep the following points in mind:

1. Quite a few mutual funds have lower requirements for initial and subsequent investments in IRAs than for ordinary accounts. They enable you easily to practice dollar-cost averaging, which we recommend for investing in funds generally.

TABLE 8-4. Distribution of Mutual Fund IRA Accounts (Including Money Market Funds) (In millions)

Investment Objective	1981	1982	1983	1984	1985	1986
Aggressive Growth	*	0.3	0.8	1.1	1.1	1.5
Growth	0.1	0.2	0.8	1.0	1.1	1.5
Growth and Income	*	0.2	0.4	0.7	0.9	1.9
Precious Metals	NA	NA	NA	NA	0.2	0.2
International	NA	NA	NA	NA	0.2	0.6
Balanced	*	*	*	*	*	0.2
Income	*	0.1	0.1	0.3	0.1	0.2
Option/Income	*	*	*	0.1	0.2	0.2
Government Income	NA	NA	NA	NA	0.5	1.0
Ginnie Mae	NA	NA	NA	NA	0.3	0.6
Corporate Bond	0.1	0.2	0.4	0.5	0.6	0.8
Money Market	0.3	1.0	1.6	2.2	2.6	3.0
Total	0.5	1.9	4.1	5.9	7.9	11.6

* Fewer than 0.1 million.
NA = not available
Totals may not add due to rounding.
Source: Investment Company Institute.

2. When you buy directly from them, no-load mutual funds entail lower fees and transaction costs, whether for IRAs or not, than most of the other institutions. It's hard to see why you'd be better off buying mutual fund shares from a bank or broker than from a no-load fund itself.

3. Since all money coming out of IRAs will be taxable when you eventually withdraw it, you will not want to invest a penny of IRA money in a tax-exempt mutual fund (or, outside a mutual fund, in tax-exempt securities).

4. If your strategy for long-term capital growth involves allocating part of your money to high-risk investments in hopes of high rewards,

it might be better to do so outside IRAs, where any capital losses can be offset against capital gains or current income.

5. The Tax Reform Act of 1986 has essentially relieved you of the need to worry about which funds to invest in within an IRA context, and which outside, inasmuch as it left short- and long-term capital gains, as well as current income, taxed at the same rate. Since taxes on income are deferred until you withdraw from your IRAs, you may wish to invest IRA money in funds offering higher yields while allocating non-IRA money to superior funds with lower yields and low portfolio turnover—that is, funds whose total returns are likely to consist principally of unrealized capital gains.

6. If you have a hard time choosing between two funds of apparently equal merit, it is desirable to select for an IRA the fund whose sponsor also offers a money market fund. The possibility of an easy switch from one to the another is especially attractive in dealing with IRAs because of the rules and procedures governing the moving of money. In directing a multi-fund company to move your IRA money from one fund to another—because you want to take less risk or because you want to take more—you are not switching trustees. Therefore, you don't need to worry about IRS regulations on such moves. (Of course, the fund company may have its own, but they tend to be fairly accommodating to encourage you to stay with them.)

7. You'll especially appreciate the ease of dealing with a superior no-load mutual fund when you're involved with IRAs. Once you fill out the proper application forms and are accepted, you can handle all of your business from the comfort of your home by mail and by telephone.

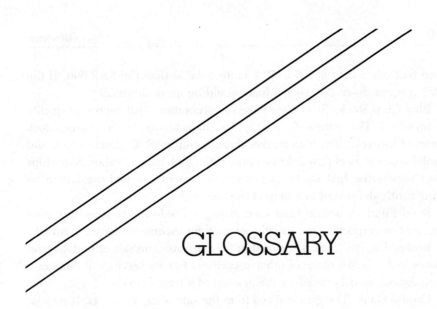

GLOSSARY

Alpha. The measure of a fund's performance in relation to its level of risk, or volatility. A fund with a positive alpha is performing better than expected. One with a negative alpha is underperforming.

Automatic Reinvestment. The choice which mutual funds provide investors with respect to distributions of dividends and capital gains. They may elect to reinvest all dividends and capital gains in additional fund shares or to reinvest only the dividends or the capital gains and get checks for the other.

Back-End Load (or Redemption Fee). A fee, ranging from about 1% to about 4%, that some mutual funds levy against investors when they redeem shares. Some are on a graduated scale that starts high and drops with each year that shares are held.

Balanced Fund. A mutual fund that has invested in a minimum percentage of bonds, preferred stocks, and/or convertible securities in addition to common stocks.

Beta. A measure of the volatility of stocks, mutual fund shares, and entire portfolios in relationship to that of the stock market, represented by the Standard & Poor's 500 Stock Price Index. The S&P has a beta of 1.0. (A riskless asset, such as a money market fund share, has a beta of 0.) A mutual fund that has a beta of 1.5 is 50% more volatile than the S&P 500. If the S&P is up or down 2%, such a fund would be up or down 3%.

Blue Chip Stock. Stocks are those of corporations that represent quality to investors. The companies usually are characterized by large size, stock prices of low volatility, high market share, a continual dividend record, and a solid balance sheet (low debt to equity ratio, high current ratio). Blue chips are typically the first stocks to recover in a recession, and the last to be significantly depressed in a market decline.

Bond Fund. A mutual fund specializing in fixed-income securities, government or corporate, and usually selected for income rather than growth.

Broker/Dealer. A firm engaged in the purchase and sale of mutual fund shares and a broad range of other securities. For its services, it charges a commission, usually based on the amount of a transaction.

Capital Gain. The gain realized from the sale of capital assets. It may be the gain in the value of an investor's holding of mutual fund shares—or in the fund's holding of stocks or other investments. The latter is distributed to the fund's shareholders. Shareholders who switch between funds within a mutual fund family incur a tax liability if they realize a gain when redeeming shares. To the tax authorities, a switch is a sale—at a gain or a loss—and a purchase.

Capital Gains Distribution. Mutual funds are required to distribute realized capital gains to their shareholders, thereby transferring to them the liability to pay any income taxes due. Shareholders must report the gains on their tax returns, whether they reinvest the money in additional shares or receive cash. Distributions are normally paid once a year.

Capitalization. The value of all the securities (principally bonds, common and preferred stocks) that constitute the capital structure of a corporation.

Cash Equivalent. Any asset that has a maturity of a year or less, such as a Treasury bill or commercial paper. Cash equivalents are regarded as a means of lowering the volatility of a mutual fund and are considered the assets with least risk and the least potential for capital gain.

Certificate of Deposit (CD). An obligation issued by a bank or savings and loan institution for terms varying from several months to a few years. CDs pay interest, but vary in financial soundness. It is, therefore, important for investors to realize that CDs with the highest relative yields may place investors at the greatest risk.

Clone Fund. A fund created by a fund management organization with the same investment objectives of another that has become successful, both in sales of shares and in performance.

Closed-end Fund. Also known as a closed-end investment company, it differs from mutual funds in that it has a specified number of shares and does not redeem them. Investors who wish to buy or to sell shares deal with one another via brokers. Unlike mutual fund shares, whose net asset value is based on the valuation of their holdings, shares of closed-end funds are traded—many on stock exchanges—at prices determined by supply and demand in the same manner as ordinary stocks or bonds.

Common Stock. The security which signifies ownership in a corporation. It is the financial asset which normally is characterized by the highest volatility—and the highest probability of gain or loss. Stockholders may receive a share of earnings, in the form of dividends, every 3 months, but are not guaranteed a cent. At a time of liquidation, they are the last to receive any money for their interest in the company.

Contractual Plan. A plan offered an investor that stipulates a schedule for buying mutual fund shares, at a stated sales charge, within a specified time.

Custodian. The qualified bank or other business organization that holds in custody the securities and other investments owned by a mutual fund.

Distributions. Payments of income dividends and realized capital gains made by mutual funds.

Diversification. An investment policy, epitomized by mutual funds, which is intended to reduce investment risks through ownership of the securities of a diverse group of industries and companies as well as diverse securities types.

Dollar-cost Averaging. An investment program that entails investment of equal amounts of cash at fixed intervals over a period of time, regardless of market conditions. Based on the assumption that it is impossible to schedule purchases in a way that is certain to obtain the lowest price, it leads to buying more shares when prices are lower and fewer shares when they are higher, and should result in lower average share prices if continued long enough.

Ex-dividend Date. The day following the day when stockholders of record are entitled to be credited with an income distribution.

Expense Ratio. The ratio of a fund's expenses to average net assets.

Incentive Compensation. An arrangement mutual funds often have with investment advisers, providing a graduated scale of payment for improved performance.

Income Dividends. Distributions to mutual fund shareholders of dividend and interest income earned on the fund's investments, less fund expenses. Depending on the fund, they are made monthly, quarterly, semiannually, or annually.

Index Fund. A mutual fund whose directive is to produce a rate of return equivalent to a market index, usually the S&P 500.

Individual Retirement Account (IRA). A vehicle created by the U.S. Government in 1974 to induce individuals to save money to supplement their expected retirement income by giving them tax incentives.

Investment Adviser. A person (company) who (which), pursuant to a contract, regularly advises a mutual fund as to how to allocate assets and what securities it should buy or sell, or is empowered actually to determine allocation, purchases and sales within the scope that is set by the fund's board of directors (trustees). To engage in interstate commerce, advisers must be registered with the Securities and Exchange Commission under the Investment Advisers Act of 1940.

Investment Company. A company—usually a corporation or a trust—formed to provide investors a vehicle for the pooling of money for investment in portfolios of securities. Mutual funds are one type of investment company.

Management Fee. The fee paid by a mutual fund to its adviser in accordance with a contract that is approved by a majority of fund shareholders.

Money Market Fund. A fund that is invested in short-term securities and is essentially riskless—albeit, not insured by the government as a bank account or as secure as a U.S. Government security except when it invests only in government issues.

Municipal Bond Fund. A fund that is invested in the bonds of cities and states. Dividends, based on interest received from the bond investments, are not taxed by the federal government.

Mutual Fund. An open-end investment company, registered with the SEC under the Investment Company Act of 1940, that issues new shares to anyone who wishes to buy them—except when sales are suspended to new investors—and always stands ready to buy them back. In providing investors the opportunity to have interests in the securities of many companies, it offers diversification, lower risk, and professional management.

Net Asset Value per Share (NAV). The gross value of a mutual fund's assets, less its liabilities, divided by the total number of its shares. Established daily, it is the price at which no-load mutual funds redeem and sell shares and the price to which load funds add a sales charge.

No-load Fund. A mutual fund which sells shares at its NAV. It does not impose a sales charge, or load. Some no-load funds do levy other fees.

Offering Price. The price at which a share of a mutual fund's stock can be bought. For no-load funds, it's the net asset value. For load funds, it's the NAV plus the load.

Open-end Investment Company. The legal term for a mutual fund.

Option. A right to buy a security (call) or to sell a security (put) at a specified price within a set period of time.

Option Income Fund. A mutual fund that sells options on stocks in its portfolio to generate supplemental income.

Over-the-Counter Market. The market consisting of a network of securities dealers in which securities are bought and sold when not traded on stock exchanges.

Performance Fund. A mutual fund that takes maximum risk to achieve maximum gain, usually short-term oriented, with very high portfolio turnover.

Portfolio. The securities of all types held by an individual investor or by an institutional investor such as a mutual fund.

Portfolio Turnover Rate. The rate at which a mutual fund turns over its portfolio securities in a year. It is calculated by dividing the lesser of sales or purchases by the monthly average value of the fund's portfolio (excluding U.S. Government securities and other securities maturing or expiring in less than 1 year). A higher turnover may mean higher brokerage commissions, higher taxable capital gains, or both.

Prospectus. The pamphlet which issuers of mutual fund shares and other securities are required by the Securities Act of 1933 to provide to every prospective purchaser. The prospectus of a mutual fund describes the fund, its investment objectives and policies, officers, directors, administrative costs, fees and charges. It also provides financial statements and instructions on how to buy and sell the fund's shares.

Redemption. Sale of shares back to the fund that issued them, directly or indirectly via a broker.

Redemption Price. The price at which a fund's shares are redeemed, usually the net asset value.

Sales Charge (or Load). A charge of up to 8.5% imposed by many mutual funds to compensate brokers who sell their shares. It is added to the net asset value.

Sector Fund. A mutual fund invested in a portfolio of common stocks concentrated in one economic sector. Such funds appeal to investors who believe that they can judge which sectors will do better than the rest of the economy and, therefore, which funds will do better than the market.

12b-1 Plan. A plan, named for an SEC rule, adopted in 1980, whereby funds impose an annual charge, usually around 1%, to recover from shareholders their costs of marketing and distribution of fund literature. A fund owner holding shares of such a fund for 12 years suffers a reduction in their net worth of 1% each year, or 12.7% compounded.

Unit Trust. An unmanaged portfolio with one liquidation date. While there are some intermediate maturity unit trusts, most average 25 years and place investors with long time horizons at significant risk.

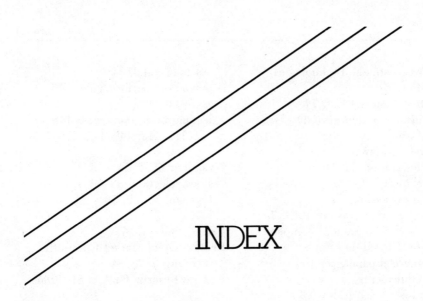

INDEX

total return compared with
mutual fund indices, 99
total return in down years, 4
use as portfolio performance
yardstick, 4n

State Street Investment
Corporation, 74
Stock funds, *see* Equity funds
Stock market crash of 1929:
impact on closed-end funds, 75
impact on mutual funds, 75
Stock market cycles:
considerations when investing,
129, 139–140
length of, 24–25
stock price swings in, 24–25
Stocks, *see also* Financial assets
attributes of, 23, 26
historic rates of return compared
with inflation, 18–20
market leadership, 182, 184–186
volatility of rates of total return,
21
Stock selection, 119
Strong Opportunity Fund, 147

Tax Reform Act of 1986:
capital gains treatment, change
in, 23, 143
encouragement of home equity
loans, 11
Individual Retirement Accounts,
change in deductibility of

annual contributions, 192,
196
pension vesting, change in, 10
Terrana, Elizabeth, 148
Tsai, Gerald, 84
Tuition, planning for, 11
12b-1 fee, 62

United Continental Income fund,
170
United Mutual Fund Selector, 51
U.S. Treasury bills, *see also* Cash
equivalents
rates of return, 18, 19, 27

Vanguard Group., Inc., 45–47
Vanguard Quantitative Portfolios,
Inc., 45–47
Vanguard Wellesley Income Fund,
143, 145
Vanguard Wellington Fund, 74
Vanguard Windsor II Fund, 44,
143, 145
Volcker, Paul A., 94–95

The Wall Street Journal, 12, 27,
68, 171
Wharton School of Finance and
Commerce (University of
Pennsylvania) study of mutual
funds, 81, 85, 87
Wiesenberger Financial Services,
52–53
Wojnilower, Albert M., 96